They Changed Me

The Transforming Power of Unconditional Love

Sherita Thompson

ISBN 978-1-0980-3611-9 (paperback)
ISBN 978-1-0980-3612-6 (digital)

Christian Faith Publishing, Inc.
832 Park Avenue
Meadville, PA 16335
www.christianfaithpublishing.com

Illustrated by Tarek Elkholy

Printed in the United States of America

*This book is dedicated with love to my husband,
Courtney, and to our three children, Josiah, James,
and Jade. Your unconditional love has
given me life, peace, hope, and joy. Thank you for loving me.*

Contents

Acknowledgments

First, I would like to thank God for giving me the strength to follow through on His divine leading and inspiration to complete my forgotten dream of writing and sharing my story of love, forgiveness, restoration, and redemption. Thank you, Lord, for helping me rediscover my ministry of sharing your unconditional love and forgiveness.

Second, I want to say a special thanks to my family. I feel incredibly blessed and fortunate to have such an amazing family at my side, cheering me on, and providing support in countless ways. I owe a debt of gratitude to my husband, not just for allowing me to be a stay-at-home mom so that I can care for and educate our children but for his selfless love, prayers, and continued sacrifices. To our children, Josiah, James, and Jade, you are the wind beneath my wings. Mommy absolutely loves and adores you. My life would not be the same without your laughter, tears, and unconditional love. I pray that each of you will use all the good you have learned from us in your own marriages, always remembering that true love always forgives and always accepts forgiveness.

Third, to my brother-in-law, Dr. Alonzo Smith, for his patience, encouragement, prayers, and unwavering support, I say a heartfelt thank you. Your support goes beyond anything I could have imagined.

ACKNOWLEDGMENTS

My dear friends, Dr. Sherieka Duncan, Juline McLean, Danieth Pryce, Edna McCalla, Antonettisha Baker, Esther Daley, Sasha McCalla, and Chinaemerem Ojevwe, your unwavering prayers and support have been a source of encouragement and inspiration to me. Thank you for keeping me grounded. Deneisa Bucknor, thanks for sticking by me when things got difficult and for reminding me that I can do anything I set my mind to with God's help.

To my friend Shauna, I don't have words to truly express how thankful and blessed I am to have you in my life. A great part of this book's success is because you gave me the most precious gift a friend can give: your time. Thank you for always understanding. Thank you for never judging me. Thank you for accepting me. Your open-mindedness and compassionate heart always comforted me. Thank you for being by my side throughout this journey and for always giving me reasons to keep writing. I am beyond blessed to call you my friend.

Finally, I would like to thank my extended family, Janet Riley and Pamela Housen for your love, support, and faithful contribution. Thank you for not squashing my dreams, but rather, you supported and encouraged me all throughout the process. Thank you for checking in on me regularly and providing feedback through this process. It was a blessing to the success of my life and ministry. Novelette McFarlane, my sister and "mother," thanks for your love, ongoing encouragement, and support. You have always been my greatest cheerleader, encouraging me to carry on whenever I grew weary and wanted to quit. This book might never have been written without your love, faithful prayers, and words of encouragement.

I will forever love and cherish each of you in my heart.

Preface

S ome people wait their entire life to find true love. For Courtney and me, we fell in love without knowing how or when. Two strangers from the same country, we knew nothing about each other until we met the summer of 2006 on the University of Maryland Eastern Shore's campus. We instantly became friends.

We had nothing in common, but love gave us everything we have ever wanted and more. My entire life, I prayed for my knight in shining armor, the one who will love me with an everlasting love, and for three years, he stood right in front of me, and I never ONCE noticed he was there.

As our friendship evolved, and his love began to pierce my heart, I found myself falling in love with my best friend. He was everything I dreamed my husband would be: loving, soft-spoken, intelligent, mild-tempered, respectful, committed, sacrificial, a perfect gentleman. But more importantly, he loved the Lord, and I needed that.

His patience was unyielding, his compassion breathtaking, and his love captivating. He was like no other man I had ever met. I knew we were meant to be together, and I knew I wanted to spend the rest of my life with him.

PREFACE

I thank the Lord for giving me the man He knows I needed to make me a better woman, a better wife, a better mom and, most importantly, a better Christian.

And thank you, Courtney, for choosing me and us.

Love always,
Your wife, Sher

Foreword

A ny book whose subject is as emotionally engaging as love is bound to leave a reader wanting more. Some individuals believe in the notion of "love at first sight," while there are those on the other end of the spectrum who don't believe that true love exists at all. It's a subject that has undoubtedly been debated throughout time, but there's enough evidence to suggest that it is really possible to find true, lifelong love when you're not searching for it.

This book is a first-hand account of one such encounter with a love that simply will not let go or give up in spite of how much it is spurned. It's a heartwarming and truly breathtaking depiction of love through the eyes and heart of my dear friend, Sherita, whose life was destined to be transformed by love—human and divine. Little did she know that the world she had grown to be perfectly satisfied with, as long as she had utter control of it all, was getting ready to be shaken immensely and turned upside down so that she could begin to experience the love of our Heavenly Father through an amazing husband and the beautiful offspring their marriage would one day produce. Little did she realize that the Most High had amazing plans to change her life forever for the better.

This journey called life is often unsuspecting as it relates to how impactful our mere existence can be upon the people within our sphere of influence. In fact, we often don't think about the ramifications of some of the decisions we make in life, and little do we realize that our actions are truly speaking much louder than our words and leaving an indelible impression upon those around us—family, friends, neighbors, associates, coworkers, and even strangers. Sherita's journey will take you through some of her own experiences, both positive and negative, that not only shaped who she is today but that also continue to shed light upon the changes that she sees our Heavenly Father making in her heart and life with each passing day.

This book is a subtle reminder that life is really not always what we want it to be. Sometimes, sadness, loneliness, emptiness, pain, and fear become accomplices and lead us down the wrong path in life. However, it's reassuring to know that Father God is completely aware of the way we take before we decide to venture down that road. I am grateful for the intriguing way in which He intercepted Sherita's life and has given her beauty for all the ashes she's been surrounded by for years because of life circumstances—loss, death, and abandonment.

I don't fully understand how or why the things a person says and does, or doesn't say or do for that matter, correlate in a positive or negative way, thereby somehow, leading to a change taking place within our hearts. Human nature, I suppose. However, I dare say that this book sheds some light on the subject as to how it's even remotely possible. It's also challenging to fathom the amazing possibilities that await us if we are willing to put self and pride aside, surrender and submit to God's leading, and allow our Heavenly Father to begin the work of transforming our heart and character from the inside out. In this case, after much resistance, Sherita slowly began to take these steps in her own life and is now reaping the benefits of answered prayers in ways that she could never have imagined possible in her wildest dreams. She now realizes that she is becoming a very different person from the one she was prior to marriage and children, and that the changes, though daunting at first, are proving to be a tremendous blessing.

Perhaps you have been resistant to the changes that our Heavenly Father desires to bring into your life. Maybe you don't think that you're the one who needs to change, but rather, that someone else does. Could it be that a stubborn will, a deceitful heart, pride, selfishness, unforgiveness, your ever-resurfacing past, and just an unwillingness to surrender to Christ's leadership are all responsible for the predicament you now find yourself in? Then again, perhaps you don't think you have a problem and that someone or something else is really the problem. If that's the case, then I am afraid that it's time for some serious introspection.

By no means is this book a figment of someone's imagination, although it may, sometimes, feel like a surreal and epic romance novel or something out of a movie. Instead, what you are about to read is a collection of amazing, mind-boggling stories about the traumas of childhood and adolescence, nestled among transparent and emotionally-charged letters to her husband (Courtney) and children (Josiah, James, and Jade), and heartfelt prayers bathed in Scripture, from the heart of a woman who knows what it means to believe in God, commune with God, and trust in the Most High God. It is not intended to give you a solution for your own marital or parental challenges in life. However, my sincere hope is that it will start you on your own journey to analyze how your past has affected and is still affecting your present. I am hoping that as you read the book, it will encourage you to purpose to do something differently about your situation that will bring positive, wholesome, lasting, and life-giving changes to you and your family.

Self-reliance can be detrimental, so as you read and come under conviction, I urge you to humble yourself and ask our wise, loving, merciful Heavenly Father to show you your true condition so that you can see your need for His divine intervention and then, in obedience, apply the antidote He recommends to bring the changes that are needed in your own life. When reality stares you squarely in the face, you must face it and deal with it, not in your own strength but in His. At different intervals, I also encourage you to stop reading and pray about things the Spirit of God reveals to your heart about yourself and about other people who you may need to approach or distance yourself from for one reason or another.

You see, our lives are but a canvas on which the Most High God wishes to paint a beautiful picture for all the world to see and experience His glory and majesty. Sherita's story is one such rendition, and it's a wonderful masterpiece by the Master Artist. I realize that all of our stories differ in so many ways and on so many levels, and because of this awareness, I have learned the importance and value of not comparing my canvas to anyone else's. Instead of wishing that some fanciful, fairytale-sounding story were mine, by God's grace, I now find myself in a place where I ask the Father to remove envy and jealousy from my heart and simply empower me with more of His Spirit so that I can nobly embrace the changes that are necessary for me to grow and mature in the areas of my life that are less than desirable.

Our Heavenly Father loves us with an everlasting love which we can NEVER fully comprehend while living here on this earth which has been so marred by sin and suffering. That same infinite love desires to see you and me live happy, joyful, fulfilling, and abundant lives in Him. Apart from Him, it's all, as it were, a charade, a moment of temporary gratification. He cares about our present day-to-day existence but is more concerned about our eternity, and how we live our lives in the here and now will certainly be telling in that regard.

So go, grab a box of tissues. Get your Bible for reference and a writing instrument. Find a cozy spot and buckle up for the journey ahead because this book promises to leave you counting your blessings and asking yourself many questions about your own journey, your walk with our Father God, and about the relationships you either hold near and dear or distant and valueless.

Once you put this book down, take heart and never forget that Father God sees each of us right where we are and understands the gravity of the situation that we face from day-to-day. Nothing takes Him by surprise; He's already "in the know." Through it all, He has a purpose and a plan to reshape the way you and I think, act, and live so that we can truly be emissaries of love, light, and life in this world of selfishness, darkness, and death. I pray that we will let Him change us for the better while we humbly and faithfully serve those around us and ever reflect the lovely, beautiful, radiant image of our Creator as we live for Him in this world.

Personally, I was tremendously blessed, motivated to make changes in my own life and, no doubt, encouraged by every story, letter, and prayer shared in the book. My prayer is that you will too and that your faith will be reignited for the rest of your journey through this life.

Love, peace, and *blessings!*

Shauna (Menns) Reid

My Story

This section is an introductory sneak preview into my life and journey and the relationships I have with my biological family, myself, my husband, and my children. It also lends to the impact that my childhood has had on who I am today as a woman, mother, wife, and daughter of the Most High God, who loves me immensely and cares deeply about me. As I reflect upon the experiences of my life, I now realize that, at every step of the way, God's hand has been upon me, and He is very much involved with everything that's transpired in my life from the time I came into this world.

And we know that all things work together
for good to them that love God, to them who
are the called according to his purpose.

— Romans 8:28

If It Were Left Up to Me, I Probably Would Not Have Chosen My Husband

"For I know the plans I have for you," declares the LORD,
"plans to prosper you and not to harm you,
plans to give you hope and a future."

—Jeremiah 29:11

The Bible is filled with individuals who, for one reason or another, felt the need to disobey God's instructions. There are also several individuals who believe they could run away from God after He gave them an assignment or specific instructions to carry out a task—Jonah, Moses, Gideon, and Jeremiah are just a few of them. One of those stories, the story of Jonah, just happens to be my favorite Bible story. The interesting thing about the story and why I love it is the outcome, and not so much the process. You see, God had a plan to save the people of Nineveh, and He decided who He would use to carry out His mission. Regardless of whether Jonah was compliant with the divine directive or not, God knew who was the BEST man for the job, and it was Jonah.

As the story reveals in the Old Testament book of Jonah, EVERY LAST ONE of the Ninevites WERE SAVED once Jonah repented of his disobedience to God, after which, he was led to bring the message God had given him to the people of Nineveh (Jonah 1–4). Perhaps I love this story so much because I can relate in so many ways to this man of God and because I realize that God often speaks to us, but many times, we either don't care to listen, or we are just uneasy or stubborn about following up with the way He desires to lead us.

In hindsight, I must admit that my own life story is a little like Jonah's. You see, God made it clear to me that my husband was the man I should marry, but like Jonah, I kept running away. Three times, I declined his attempted proposal, finding every excuse I could come up with to avoid the process. I fussed about the rings and complained that I didn't love the rings because they were either too expensive (I wasn't even the one paying for them), too flashy, or they were just not made up of the right material (I made sure that he knew that I didn't like white gold). Oh man, wow! The strange thing was that I genuinely loved him and knew in my heart that he was the man I wanted to spend the rest of my life with. I know you're probably thinking that I must have been crazy to make such statements in response to his honest, loving attempts at proposing to me. Right? I know that it might even seem a little contradictory for me to say that I love him since I kept declining his proposals. But it's true, and I knew it.

No one can truly understand the gravity of my past pain because I am not able to put everything into words; some things I have had to leave at the secret throne of God. Conversely, not everyone will be able to fully understand my praise.

Throughout my life, I have had some amazing experiences and equally amazing people who supported me on my journey—individuals who sacrificed their time and invested their money so that I could advance my education and career, individuals who loved me and wanted to see me succeed, individuals who believed in me before I knew what it meant to believe in myself or who kept on believing in me during times when I stopped believing in myself, individuals who gave me a home in their heart so that I could experience love. I do not have words to truly express my undying gratitude to each and every one of them.

Amid all these wonderful blessings, I would be lying if I didn't mention that there were days, if not months, probably even years, at different intervals throughout my life, when I experienced feelings of hopelessness and despair. There were many days when I wished the nights would never end so that I wouldn't have to face the ridicules of bullying at school—I didn't know that was what it was called then. Years of feeling unloved and unworthy; years of feeling rejected and unwanted, even though I fully recognized that my life wasn't the worst—that didn't change or take away the pain my heart was feeling. But it was during some of those difficult seasons that I felt God's hands on my life. I will tell you, that is the only reason I survived.

Interestingly enough, although I recognized that God was the *one* protecting me, I didn't really know Him personally. I always read my Bible, prayed, and occasionally attended church, but I didn't have the greatest relationship with Him. So I kept going back into the proverbial driver's seat, always taking "control" of my life, never truly relinquishing control and fully trusting God to lead me. Hence, my feeble attempt at trying to control my future.

> *"For I know the plans I have for you,"*
> *declares the Lord, "plans to prosper you and*
> *not to harm you, plans to give you hope and*
> *a future." (Jeremiah 29:11)*

This attitude of wanting to be in control and not being willing to submit extended itself into my marriage and caused a lot of unnecessary pain. When I was a child, God's hands were on my life, and in adulthood, I realized that His hands were still on me and my marriage even after all I had endured. It took me almost seven years to truly accept, beyond a shadow of a doubt, that my life and marriage were absolutely where God needed me to be even though God had given me/us the confirmation before we got married.

You might ask: Why so long? Or what was the confirmation?

Well, first, I kept on living in the past and refused to accept my present and future. Additionally, whenever things got difficult, I would question God about whether my husband is truly my life partner. I also had false ideations and expectations about marriage, mine included. I thought it was supposed to be perfect—not sure where I got that idea from. I didn't know that married couples argue and "fight," and if they did that, it was such a constant thing. So whenever we disagreed on issues, I just didn't know what to do, and before long, a small issue could explode into something bigger.

I also knew that he made me angry, and I annoyed him plenty as well. We seldom agreed on financial matters, but we are working on this now. We have very different parenting styles, in that, he is calm and relaxed, a little too relaxed for me at times. I, on the other hand, am forceful and require way too much perfection from my children. He is messy, and I am USED to being borderline obsessive compulsive; however, having children changed that. He is a planner and very detail-oriented, and I live life on "crazy" faith. These are some of our differences, to name a few. It's been said that "opposites attract," and we are truly the complete opposite of each other; it's beautifully chaotic.

Time and time again, I asked God if He was sure Courtney was the man I was supposed to spend the rest of my life with. But the answer wasn't coming, and so I kept on asking. You see, we like when God works according to our timing, but He doesn't, either because we are not mature enough to accept His answer(s), or because He can't trust us with the truth.

However, that all changed during one of my complaining sessions to God. This time, it wasn't during my devotional time; no, it was while I was taking a shower. After all, it's the only place where I find a bit of quiet these days. He showed me why He ordained my marriage to the man I now call my best friend, confidant, and husband. In an effort to make sure I did not forget, I turned off the shower and picked up my phone and wrote His answer down.

In the most loving and heartwarming way, He said: *"Courtney is the vessel that I used to save you. By marrying Courtney, I have saved you from a life of perpetual sinning, a life of bondage, a life without direction and purpose, a life of compromising, a life of accepting less than you deserve, a life of wants, a life of betrayal, a life of settling, and a life of lying."*

Prior to meeting my husband, I lived a life contrary to the calling of God. Once we began dating, I rededicated my heart to God, and one year later, I recommitted my life to Him through baptism.

Like God, who is persistent in His love for us and not wanting any of us to perish but desiring everyone to come to repentance (2 Peter 3:9), my future husband was persistent and steadfast in his chase and love of his future bride. As we reflect upon Jonah's life, God would not allow his temporary disobedience to derail His plans of saving the people of Nineveh. In the same manner, it was God's plan to save me all along through my husband's love and persistence. I am thankful God was persistent.

My husband is far from perfect as you can tell, but so am I. But this life is not about who is perfect; it is about God and His Kingdom. It is about saving us. God will use the most uncomfortable situations or the person you least expect to bring you into His fold. Thank God for my husband.

So when your marriage feels like an uphill battle, when nothing is going the way you imagined or planned, I pray that you won't be like Jonah or me and run away or try to hide or avoid the inevitable. Take time to remember the bondage God took you from and ask Him to open your eyes so that you can see the blessing in the spouse He has gifted you with. Search your heart, search your soul, and when you are done searching, decide whether or not your marriage is worth fighting for.

Trust in the Lord with all your heart, and lean not on your own understanding; In all your ways acknowledge Him, and He shall direct your paths. (Proverbs 3:5–6)

God's Perfect Plan

If you believe, you will receive whatever you ask for in prayer.

—Matthew 21:22

Our Steps Are Ordered by the Lord

I am the youngest of twenty-three siblings, so, family is very important to me. We did not all live together, but my family was still very close-knit. Unfortunately, tragedy struck when I was only seven years old. My mother got sick, and within three months, she passed away. My world, as I remembered it, was shattered, and the next nine years would be, undeniably, the most painful and difficult years of my life. I found myself living anywhere and with anyone who I believed would love me, and would provide a stable home for me, but I never found true love or a stable home. I was often left heartbroken, feeling unloved and unwanted. The physical, emotional, and verbal abuse inflicted upon me at the hands of those who were supposed to love and protect me left me feeling incapacitated. It was during those days, when life seemed darkest, that I made a vow that if I ever became a mother, I would do everything in my power to make sure my children never feel the way I did. I promised myself that I would never ask anyone to care for my children out of fear that they might mistreat or subject them to the gross maltreatment I experienced as a child.

This instability robbed me of my childhood, and it forced me to grow up quickly. My brain quickly went into survival mode. I felt like I had to protect myself and all the children around me, and at sixteen years old, I decided I wanted to help children who are from broken homes and families. This led me to pursue the teaching profession, but two years into my teaching degree, I realized that it was not my calling, and that was not where God wanted me to be. Just before finishing up my undergraduate degree, I was introduced to counseling by my then friend, and now my husband, Courtney. It was in the very first class of my graduate studies that my life changed forever. I found my purpose! I am going to be a counselor! I can finally be the voice for those children who are hurting. I can finally be the voice that will speak on their behalf and protect them from the cruel mistreatment of those who are supposed to protect them.

My World Was Once Again Shattered

In January 2009, four months before my graduation, I got the worst phone call of my life.

It was the Sabbath! I was excited because I was heading to church, and I couldn't wait to share my encounter with God a few hours earlier. But then my phone rang. It was my brother, and at the sight of his name, my heart plummeted into the pit of my stomach. I hesitantly picked up the phone, and before the salutation was over, his voice said, "DADDY DIED THIS MORNING AT AROUND 3 A.M." My knees buckled beneath me. The silence on the phone was deafening. I felt nauseated. The air felt like it left my body momentarily because I couldn't breathe. I lost my father to Cancer. My world, once organized and well-planned, was shattered once again. You see, my father was my everything. My life, and everything I did, revolved around him. I worked for him and went to school for him. I was supposed to take care of him the way he took care of me, but now, all that was gone. I realized that I would never get to show him how much I appreciated what he did for me.

The pain was indescribable, and the loss unbearable. It was then that Courtney became my tower of strength. He was my ever-present shoulder to lean on and to cry on, my ever-present friend. He invited me to church and made himself available at whatever hour I needed him. He also took the time to explain and clarify anything I studied from the Scriptures. His love and compassion were heart-warming, and his patience was refreshing. As the months passed, I found myself falling in love with my best friend, but the loss of my father was still very difficult for me emotionally and I needed a way out. I needed a way to escape my pain, so, getting married and having a family became my focus. Furthermore, having a family was a lifelong dream of mine anyhow.

The Two Became One

Therefore what God has joined together,
let no one separate.

—Mark 10:9

Faith Brought Us Together and
God Sealed Us for Eternity

Growing up, I knew I wanted to marry someone who was a Christian and someone who loves the Lord. I met Courtney in 2006, while attending university in the USA, and we became instant friends, even though we had nothing in common, except that we were both Jamaicans. He was polite and friendly, charming, intelligent, handsome, and a Christian. I, on the other hand, was an athlete, loud, witty, insensitive but friendly, outgoing, talkative, and 100 percent certain Courtney was not the man of my dreams. However, while in graduate school, we found ourselves spending more time together, and our conversations lasting for hours, but still, no expressed affection was shared.

So, in 2010, we decided to start dating. We dated for two years before Courtney proposed. I can't say it was a smooth-sailing experience for Courtney, because I recall him purchasing three different sets of wedding rings — all of which I had a problem with because of fear, leading up to the day I said I would marry him. I knew I loved him, but I wasn't sure if I was the right woman for him. He was, and still is, charming, loving, hardworking, committed, sacrificial, patient, gentle, and loyal. These are all positive traits, and the qualities I wanted and needed in a husband, but I wasn't sure if I deserved all that, or even if I deserved a man like him. So, I decided to put God to the test, and I told Him that if Courtney was the man, he wanted me to spend the rest of my life with, then He would have to make it clear to me. I told God I needed a Gideon experience.

Statement to God: *"If during worship tomorrow night, Courtney says he is not taking the job in West Virginia (He really wanted this job and was super excited), then I know for a fact that he is the man You want me to marry."*

Fast forward to worship the next night. As we greeted each other and inquired about each other's day, Courtney said to me, "So, after thinking about everything, I decided not to move forward with the job in West Virginia." My heart was overwhelmed with joy to the point of tears. Did God just answer my prayer that quickly? I immediately shared my prayer request with him, and he responded by saying, "I asked God to give me a sign as well. I wanted to make sure I was making the right decision as well, since you kept hesitating. His answer is clear. You are the woman I will marry." Our faith was sealed for eternity from that very moment.

> *"For I know the thoughts I think toward you,"* says the Lord, *"thoughts of peace and not of evil, to give you a future and a hope."*
> (Jeremiah 29:11)

Answered Prayers

On December 12, 2012, the Lord answered my childhood dream prayer, and I got married to my best friend, the man of my dreams. A few short months later, we were expecting our first bundle of joy. But, nine weeks into my first trimester, we lost our first pregnancy to a miscarriage. I was devastated. A part of me wanted to be angry with God because I couldn't understand why He kept taking everyone I loved away from me. But our Heavenly Father was gracious to me and to us, and within a month of losing our first baby, we conceived our second child — Josiah. In May of 2014, we welcomed our first son. In September of 2016, our second son – James, was born, and in June of 2018, our unexpected miracle baby girl – Jade, entered this world.

Motherhood

Life was crazy, busy, joyful, overwhelming, and stressful, with many sleepless nights and many nights where I cried myself to sleep because I was simply overwhelmed from the day's "fight" with my children, and my perceived husband's lack of support.

My life as a wife and mother was nothing like I had dreamed it would be. It was difficult, overwhelming, and downright stressful most of the time. It shouldn't be this hard, I felt. No one told me it would be so daunting and wearisome. I believed wholeheartedly that it would be easy, that my children would be "perfect," that my husband would be "perfect," that he would be more hands-on with the children, and that life would be simple.

I began to get frustrated, extremely impatient, angry, and I shouted more than I spoke calmly. Nothing was going the way I dreamed or imagined. My heart was being broken from the constant arguments with my husband about how I discipline the children, about our finances, about me working outside the home, about me being the cause of our children's behaviors. I was disappointed in myself. How could I have gotten it so wrong? I prayed for and with my children every day. I arose early in the mornings and studied the Word of God. I/we had nightly worship with the children, and I even fasted occasionally. Am I being punished for my past sins? Am I not thankful for all the blessings God has given me? A thousand thoughts filled my head each day, and time seemed to be my worst enemy.

This is not who I was. I didn't like who I had become, and I wanted so badly to change for them, to be the best wife and mom to and for them, but every day, I felt like I failed them. I watched my children's behaviors get progressively worse. I watched myself become isolated from my husband, and I gave up on praying. What's the sense, I mused, when nothing is changing.

Self-inflicted Hopelessness

But the worst was yet to come. Self-inflicted hopelessness, disappointment, and constant criticism led me down a path to self centeredness and a critical spirit. No longer was my husband worthy of my respect or love. Absolutely nothing he did was ever good enough. I couldn't keep on top of the laundry. My house was and still is a constant mess. I am used to my house being clean and in order. You could say I have a touch of obsessive-compulsive disorder (OCD). Sometimes, I can barely get dinner on the table. As soon as I get on top of organizing our home, my husband says we are moving again.

The worst nightmare from my childhood has caught up to me again.

I love our growing family, but all too often, I find out that I am too tired and overwhelmed to show them that love in the way I want to, or in the way they deserve. The phrase "I'm not cut out for motherhood" was quickly becoming my motto and my daily taunt. My heart was breaking. My children's behaviors had also become a major focal point for me. I had taken my eyes off God. The emptiness in my heart was one that my husband couldn't fill. I needed God, and I needed Him right away. What am I going to do? I pondered. I cannot let this escalate any further.

The Disappointment and Revelation

This self-professed perfectionist hit rock bottom. It was only then that the Holy Spirit led me to Psalm 37:23–25, which says, "The Lord makes firm the steps of the one who delights in him; though he may stumble, he will not fall, for the Lord upholds him with his hand; I was young and now I am old, yet I have never seen the righteous forsaken or their children begging bread."

In that moment, I was reminded of God's perfect love. In that moment, I rededicated my heart to my first true love. In that moment, I was reminded that "there is therefore now no condemnation to those who are in Christ Jesus, who do not walk according to the flesh, but according to the Spirit" (Romans 8:1). It was in that moment that God revealed His perfect plan for my life, and in that moment, my lifelong dream was born.

Seven years and three beautiful children later, God is still at the center of our marriage. Being a wife and mom takes considerable work and time, and life isn't always perfect, but what is? There are days when we struggle with communication, parenting, and discussing financial matters, which often seems like an uphill battle, and then there is the obvious need for spending quality time together, because three children in five years can take a toll on a relationship. However, I would not trade a single moment of my life with my husband for anything this world has to offer.

But, whenever life gets overwhelming, and the "burden of perplexity and care meets us head on," it is in those moments that we encourage each other to be all that is possible for each other. It is in those moments that we often sit down and reflect on what drew us together — the long conversations, the movies about royalty, and the silly jokes whereby he bewitched me by telling me about my love languages, and I fell for it. It is in those moments that we make every effort to encourage each other while figuring out how to conquer the battles of life. It is in those moments that we hold fast to God's precious promises:

> *And surely I am with you always, to the*
> *very end of the age.* (Matthew 28:20)

> *I will instruct you and teach you in the way*
> *you should go; I will counsel you and watch*
> *over you.* (Psalm 32:8)

So, as we continue to study how to advance the happiness of each other, we see that God's plan is perfect, even though we are not. And while we continue to navigate this marriage phenomenon and continue to learn each other's complex character, as it was impossible to learn during the dating period, we work purposefully to make Christ first, last, and best in everything. With that, we believe that as our love for

Him increases, our love for eachother will grow deeper and stronger.

> *For we are His workmanship, created in Christ Jesus for good works, which God prepared beforehand that we should walk in them.* (Ephesians 2:10)

Why I Pray for My Husband

By wisdom a house is built, and through understanding
it is established. Through knowledge its rooms
are filled with rare and beautiful treasures.

—Proverbs 24:3–4

Our marriage was strong, and we had a consistent prayer life, as we perceived it. But a few months after giving birth, we relocated to Florida for my husband's new job. A mere few days after "settling" into our new home, he began working. I was left to do all the unpacking, cleaning, organizing, etc., while caring for our four-month-old baby. I was overwhelmed, miserable, frustrated, and tired. Every time I attempted to communicate how I was feeling, we would get into an argument, and before I knew it, we weren't talking about the elephant in the room any longer because "peace" was more important than the actual reality. The silent frustration began to grow, and before I knew it, our prayer life also began to suffer.

After about six months of living in our new home, my husband came home one evening and said we were moving again. It was then that I realized I needed a way to cope, so that I didn't grow resentful of my husband's "lack of sensitivity." I knew and I understood that some things were out of his control, due to the nature of his job. But I didn't think that he was compassionate about my plight. And from there, I watched myself evolve into the wife I never thought or wanted to be — the complaining wife. I found myself hating the very job that provided for us. I hated the long hours he worked. Everything he did bothered me. I was out of control, and I knew I needed to get a grip of myself. One day, as I was complaining in my head, the Holy Spirit impressed upon my heart that if I prayed for my husband as much as I complained about him, our lives would be so much better! I was angry. Why do I have to be the one to pray for him? However, I quickly learned that praying for my husband was much more effective than complaining.

> *Ask and it will be given to you; seek and you will find; knock and the door will be opened to you. For everyone who asks receives; the one who seeks finds; and to the one who knocks, the door will be opened.*
> (Matthew 7:7–8)

It was then that I made the commitment to God that I would pray for my husband, even when I did not want to or feel like praying for him. When I was angry with him, or even if my personal prayer life wasn't where it needed to be, I would still pray for him. That was four years ago. I have stayed true to that commitment, but it hasn't been easy, and I will admit that there were times when I did not want to pray for him, times when I wanted him to experience hardship, so that he could learn, times when I grew impatient and felt it was a waste of my time, because I didn't see any changes. I know it sounds awful, but it is true.

Today, my husband is a better man. Today, he is a better and more hands-on dad. Today, he is a better husband, because I prayed and still pray for him, even when I don't want to. I am not trying to take credit for the changes God has wrought in him, but I am saying prayer works. We still have a lot of growing to do, but it is important to celebrate the small victories, because the things that still need improvement can distract us. It is important to celebrate the small victories so that we can give hope to others. And it is even more important to celebrate the small victories so that we can remember to glorify God when we are tested, and when we experience challenges in the future. But even more importantly, we have to celebrate the small victories as a way of sharing God's redeeming love with others.

> *They, without a word, may be won over by the behavior of their wives.* (1 Peter 3:1–2)

I am thankful that I did not give up when I didn't see any progress, because those were probably the times when he was struggling the most and in need of me to lift him up to the Lord, because he was too "weak" to do it himself. I am thankful that I didn't stop praying, because by praying for my husband, I, too, was changed. And the most important lesson I learned is that wives who submit themselves to the Lord can have the power to change their husbands, as well as the atmosphere of their home.

So, let us "be kind and compassionate to one another, forgiving eachother, just as in Christ God forgave you" (Ephesians 4:32), and "let us not become weary in doing good, for at the proper time we will reap a harvest if we do not give up" (Galatians 6:9).

Our Journey

This section is a compilation of letters to Courtney. It captures the ups and downs and some of the deep-seated emotions of our hearts that were, sometimes, so overwhelming that they almost cost us our relationship. God had a plan though. Fueled by faith, an avowed commitment until death, and driven by His steadfast love for us and His desire to see us succeed, we weathered the storms together and have lived to tell the tale.

By wisdom a house is built, and through understanding it is established; through knowledge, its rooms are filled with rare and beautiful treasures.

—*Proverbs 24:3–4*

I Never Really Knew You

My darling Courtney,

What joy it gives me to write you this letter. I waited my entire life for you, and there you were right in front of me, but I never really knew you. You were just another friend, someone I enjoyed talking to. I remember the first time we met. I locked myself out of my apartment, and you were the graduate assistant on call. You closed the office and walked with me to my apartment room. This was uncommon and outside the standard lockout protocol, but because you were the only one in the office, you made an exception, which, I believe, was God's divine intervention. You stood outside my bedroom door, and we spoke for what felt like almost two hours. It was then that our unbreakable friendship was forged.

Looking back, I could see God's hand at work in our friendship because we would spend hours talking about life, our rich Jamaican culture, and our past and present relationships. It's interesting, as I recall our conversations, because we had absolutely nothing in common. During the summer breaks, you would visit me at my apartment and just sit around asking me questions about my love for track and field or whatever else you could conjure up to make conversation or to pass the time.

It was almost naïve to think that I did not notice your keen interest in all aspects of my life though it was obvious that you sincerely cared for me, but I honestly did not, and I certainly did not see you in my future. But as the years passed, your attention to my happiness began to slowly tug at my heart, and slowly, I let my heart unbend. And even though I felt like you were the one for me, I couldn't let go of my past memories because they "held" me down. But I knew I had to forget my first love and fall in love again.

I will never forget the moment I realized I was in love with you. My palms got wet, and an overwhelming sense of warmth took over my entire body. That afternoon, I walked to your apartment unbeknown to you, that I was coming over, and when I shared with you, what I was feeling, you refused to entertain my advances. Instead, you told me you would wait until I was completely sure a relationship with you was what I wanted. It was confirmed; I was in love with you.

I didn't know it then, but it makes sense now. As I revisit the times we hung out and replay our conversations in my head, I realize the many things I love about you: the way your eyes glitter when you look at me as if I am the only woman that exists, how handsome you look when you smile back at me, your attention to detail, whenever I am dressed for an "outing" how you take the time to make sure everything fits perfectly in place, the way you hold my hand when we are out in public, the way you cry when you think of the ones you miss, your willingness to drop whatever you are doing for me, and the way you make me laugh even when I don't feel like it. All these gestures showed me that you were the one for me. Can you imagine the fluttery feelings in my heart every time I think of you? These thoughts of you give me a warm sensation in my chest, and I happily sigh, knowing that I have you.

As our relationship grew, I would catch myself daydreaming about you kissing me, and then I would smile again at what I imagine you are thinking about me. Even now, as I am writing this letter to you, I find myself smiling with a few tears in between because of the joy my heart is feeling. To have denied this would be like denying that blood runs through my veins. I am happy I took the plunge with you. You, my love, are my safe place.

I just want to tell you every day when we wake up together in the morning, and every night before we fall asleep, that I love you. Today, I am a happy woman because I have found my one true love in you.

Love always,
Your wife, Sher

Personal Application

CONVICTION *from the Scriptures:*

> *I have found him whom my soul loves.*
> (Song of Solomon 3:4)

> *Many waters cannot quench love; rivers
> cannot wash it away. If one were to give all
> the wealth of his house for love, it would be
> utterly scorned.* (Song of Solomon 8:7)

> *This is the* LORD*'s doing; it is marvelous in
> our eyes.* (Psalm 118:23)

> *Let him kiss me with the kisses of his mouth,
> for your love is more delightful than wine.*
> (Song of Solomon 1:2)

> *Who can find a virtuous woman? for her
> price is far above rubies. The heart of her
> husband doth safely trust in her, so that he
> shall have no need of spoil. She will do him
> good and not evil all the days of her life.*
> (Proverbs 31:10–12)

COMMITMENT *from this day forward:*

I promise to never forget the first time we ever kissed,
or the moment we had our very first real kiss on our wedding
day. I still get those butterfly trips whenever I think of that
kiss. My lips and my heart belong to you alone, always! I

promise to cherish every moment I have with you—good or bad, until I take my very last breath.

CHARGE *to Readers:*

As you reminisce on the initial moments of the relationship with your spouse, may your love be as the flame of the Lord as Solomon expressed in Song of Solomon 8:6, "Place me like a seal over your heart, like a seal on your arm; for love is as strong as death, its jealousy unyielding as the grave. It burns like blazing fire, like a mighty flame." May you be the seal upon each other's heart and arm.

READER's *action plan for today:*

Write three things you loved most about your spouse when you initially began dating or courting and the emotions that describe how you felt about him or her.

1. _____

2. _____

3. _____

I Am Sorry I Hurt You

My beloved Courtney,

This letter was the most difficult to write because I did not know where to begin, or how to put into words how truly sorry I am but, at the same time, thankful for every experience we have shared, both individually and as a couple. There were so many emotions going through my head as I penned my thoughts, feelings of regret, remorse, anger—some, toward you but, mostly, at myself—guilt and just sheer sadness at the thought of some of the things I put you through. But as I look back at our journey and how it unfolded and is still unfolding, I am grateful I got to share it with you.

We have had so many disappointments, but we have also had many victories, and at each stage, I often wondered why you were ever so patient with me. Until now, I never truly realized just how blessed I was to have you in my life. If it had been me, I would have walked away from you a thousand times. But your love was pure and unyielding, and you were and still remain the same throughout all our ups and downs. Just thinking about all the pain I caused you breaks my heart. I am so blessed that you always accepted me for who I am even though it was sometimes hard. You sacrificed everything for us and risked it all, knowing you would lose so much by choosing to share your heart and life with me; nonetheless, you did it. I don't believe that I can ever repay you, but I sincerely hope my commitment to you and our life together will be an adequate demonstration of my love for you.

I am sorry for having lied to you so many times. I knew that what I was doing was wrong, but somehow,

I just couldn't stop myself. I am sorry I did not accept responsibility for my actions or admit that my behaviors negatively affected you and our relationship. Looking back now, I see how my actions broke down the fabric of our relationship and put our pending marriage in jeopardy. However, I really want to thank you for not allowing my temporary insanity or selfishness to dictate your feelings or influence your decisions. Instead, you lovingly forgave me and asked me to marry you.

I am sorry I set such unrealistic expectations for you. I unknowingly set you up to fail. I admit that I did not know how to earnestly seek God for myself, or how to present my needs and wants to Him for myself, but instead, I kept looking to you to be perfect in all things. The love I desired, needed, and was seeking is a kind of love that no man can ever give to me. I did not know it then.

During those times of mistrust, I am thankful we remained faithful. During those moments of regret, I am thankful we remained insightful. During those times when we said hurtful things to each other, I am thankful we were still able to remain peaceful. During those moments when the hurt was unbearable, I am thankful we remained prayerful. And during those times when we were doubtful, I am thankful we remained hopeful and convinced.

Secretly, you have taken the broken pieces of my heart and put them back together, very much like the jigsaw puzzles you love to do. Our troubled times were those when my heart was not put completely back together, and I was emotionally and spiritually immature. I wanted so much from you but was unwilling to sacrifice much in return. Once the last piece of the proverbial puzzle was in place, that was when I realized you were divinely assigned to be in my life in an extraordinary way. You're nothing short of an angel sent to me!

It brings tears to my eyes when I think about the many times I could have lost you because I was foolish enough to think that I could survive without you. In retrospect, I cannot imagine living life without you, then or now. I wish I could give you back the time we have lost, but since I cannot, I promise to spend my entire lifetime making it up to you. Please forgive me for not realizing sooner that every sign was pointing straight to you as the perfect one for me.

I remember daydreaming about a fairy-tale life. I remember wishing for the perfect life. But no longer do I desire those things. For today, all I want is a steady hand to lead me and a kind soul to love me, and I have found that in you. Today, I simply want someone who knows the depth and meaning of true love and is willing to sacrifice his life for his one true love. Today, I want to fall asleep and wake up knowing my heart is safe. Thank God, I know my heart is forever safe with you. Every day we are together is the GREATEST GIFT from God. So as our journey progresses and continues to unfold, just remember, I will forever be yours. The fairy tale has become a breathtaking reality on so many levels, and I thank God for sending me you.

Love always,
Sher

Personal Application

CONVICTION *from the Scriptures:*

> *For I know my transgressions, and my sin is always before me. Surely you desire truth in the inner parts; you teach me wisdom in the inmost place. Create in me a pure heart, O God, and renew a steadfast spirit within me.* (Psalm 51:3, 6, 10)

> *I have been crucified with Christ and I no longer live, but Christ lives in me. The life I now live in the body, I live by faith in the Son of God, who loved me and gave himself for me.* (Galatians 2:20)

> *Take heed to yourself. If your brother sins against you, rebuke them; and if they repent, forgive them. Even if they sin against you seven times in a day and seven times come back to you saying "I repent," you must forgive them.* (Luke 17:4)

COMMITMENT *from this day forward:*

Today, I pledge my commitment to you and our family. I know I won't always be perfect because I don't think I can be, but I try to strive, as closely as I possibly can, to be honest and true in loving you. Today, I aspire to give my very best self to you and to trust God with the process called "us." My deepest yearning is for us to live each for the other as we both live for the Lord. May the Lord cause our love to increase and overflow for each other (Philippians 1:9) through His divine grace. I sincerely pray that my life will enrich yours as it should because whoever finds a wife finds a good thing, and the Lord favors him (Proverbs 18:22).

CHARGE *to Readers:*

If, like me, you find yourself wandering or falling short in your relationship with your spouse, do not be afraid to humbly seek his or her forgiveness. Ask for God's pardon because "If we confess our sins, He is faithful and just to forgive us our sins, and to cleanse us from all unrighteousness" (1 John 1:9). Our Lord will abundantly pardon and restore you to His grace.

READER's *action plan for today:*

List three things you would like to work on in your marriage with your spouse, then ask your spouse to join you in praying to God and asking for His forgiveness.

1. _____

2. _____

3. _____

Permission to Dream

My dear husband,

Growing up as a child, I dreamed so that I could escape my past. I dreamed because I wanted a better life. I dreamed so that I could escape my reality, and so that my reality wouldn't become my destiny. I dreamed because I believed in my dreams. I dreamed-because I found hope in my dreams. I dreamed because I believed with my whole heart that God was directing my dreams.

Looking back over my life, I can clearly see how my pain has shaped my dreams. Although my dreams were many, my greatest dream was to be the sole caretaker of my mini-mes. Falling in love with you has allowed me to watch my virtual childhood dreams blossom from my head and my heart into my reality.

Loving you has allowed me to look beyond my past and to hope for a better future. Loving you has allowed me to love freely knowing that my heart will always be protected. Loving you allows me to live out my dream of being the sole-caretaker of my mini-mes. Loving you has given me the kind of peace that passes all understanding despite the occasional struggles we face in our marriage. And even when things got tough, you did not waver on your promises to make sure my dream would always be my reality.

Loving you has given me great joy, especially knowing that we have endeavored to place God at the center of our lives. Loving you has given me security, and it is heartwarming to know that I have a stable home and a husband who loves his family more than his own life. Loving you has given me a family that accepts me, cares for me, and is willing to sacrifice time and money without reservation just to see me smile.

You are long-suffering, patient, and kind. You gave us (the kids and me) all of you, leaving nothing behind. You sacrifice all your free time to be with us, never leaving us behind but always thinking of us first. You loved me even when you did not feel loved and when my imperfections caused you so much stress. You loved me when I disobeyed your requests. I know that I am complicated, but you still accepted me and love me in spite of my shortcomings.

As I cuddle my sweet babies in the early mornings, I can't help but thank God I do not have to rush off to work. All of that is possible because you have allowed me to live out my greatest dream: to be the sole caretaker of our mini-mes. I dared to dream, and my dream is now a reality because I have been so graciously blessed by God because of you. Thank you!

Love always,
Your wife, Sher

Personal Application

CONVICTION *from the Scriptures:*

> *There is no fear in love. But perfect love drives out fear, because fear has to do with punishment. The one who fears is not made perfect in love.* (1 John 4:18)

> *Let no one seek his own interests, but each of you to the interests of the others.* (Philippians 2:4)

> *Do not be anxious about anything, but in every situation, by prayer and petition, with thanksgiving, present your requests to God.* (Philippians 4:6)

COMMITMENT *from this day forward:*

I know that you already know, but I will say it resoundingly again, you have fulfilled my joy by allowing me the privilege to exclusively care for our kids. My heart is satisfied in knowing that "God is not unjust; He will not forget your work and the love you have shown" to us (Hebrews 6:10).

CHARGE *to Readers:*

If, for some reason, your dreams have been cast aside because other priorities seem to be vying for your attention, then it's time to give yourself the opportunity to dream once again. Our Heavenly Father has wonderful plans in store for your life, so today, I encourage you to think of where your dreams can take you and how they can impact the lives of those around you for good. Put your hope and faith and trust in God. Remember that many are the plans in a man's heart, but it is God who orders his steps.

READER's *action plan for today:*

Think about and list some of the dreams you may have buried or put aside that you sometimes wish you could have seen come to fruition. Pray about them and, by God's grace, determine which one you can still make a reality with His help and guidance.

1. _____

2. _____

3. _____

Trials

My darling husband,

I finally understand that trials are one of God's chosen methods of training us, and part of His divine plan for our success. Believe it or not, trials are one of God's gifts to us. They are meant to draw us closer to God and closer to each other. Trials teach us to trust God and each other unconditionally. It teaches us to rely on each other. Trials push us to seek God and pray together, ensuring we fulfill God's divine plan for oneness in our marriage. I have come to see and understand that God also permits trials in an effort to refine those defective characteristics that separate us from him and each other.

It is safe to say we have had our fair share of trials, but I am grateful for every one of them, and more importantly, I am grateful that we went through them together and will continue to go through them with the Lord by our sides. Reflecting on the past six years, there were many times when we were confronted by obstacles and tested by trials and difficulties that caused us to question whether our marriage was God's divine plan. But the temporary questioning was due to our lack of maturity and faith as well as the temporary emotional anguish we experienced due to unmet and unrealistic expectations that we had, no doubt, placed upon each other.

Added to the challenges that we were confronted with on an ongoing basis was the blending of two lives from two different "worlds." This proved to be the most difficult undertaking, at times, but somehow, we made it, and we are better individuals because of our experiences. Then there were days when we said some hurtful things that caused us pain and brought feelings of distrust because one or both of us did not believe the other person was thinking of the best interest of the family. There were days when we harbored grievances toward each other because of miscommunication or lack of communication. And then there were days when we allowed PRIDE to prevent us from saying, "I am sorry. Please forgive me, because I have sinned against you and God."

Then there were those trials that were self-inflicted because we were disobedient and unwilling to yield to the instructions of the Holy Spirit. We were stubborn and unwilling to put our selfishness aside long enough to listen to each other and work together. And there were those trials that happened because we knowingly chose to go against the governing principles that we live by as Christians. But through it all, I am thankful we kept God at the center of our lives and marriage and that we remained faithful to each other, never once giving up on our marriage.

Love always,
Your wife, Sher

Personal Application

CONVICTION *from the Scriptures:*

> *We are pressed on all sides, but not crushed;*
> *perplexed, but not in despair; persecuted,*
> *but not forsaken; struck down, but not*
> *destroyed.* (2 Corinthians 4:8–9)

> *Beloved, think it not strange concerning*
> *the fiery trial which is to try you, as though*
> *some strange thing happened unto you:*
> *but rejoice, inasmuch as ye are partakers*
> *of Christ's sufferings; that, when His glory*
> *shall be revealed, Ye may be glad also with*
> *exceeding joy.* (1 Peter 4:12–13)

> *I have heard your prayer and seen your*
> *tears; I will heal you.* (2 Kings 20:5)

> *Cast your burden on the LORD, and he*
> *will sustain you; he will never permit the*
> *righteous to be moved.* (Psalm 55:22)

> *As for me, I shall call upon God, and the*
> *LORD will save me. Evening and morning*
> *and at noon, I will complain and murmur,*
> *and He will hear my voice. He will redeem*
> *my soul in peace from the battle* which is
> *against me.* (Psalm 55:16–18)

COMMITMENT *from this day forward:*

I don't know how we were able to think clearly during some of those difficult times, and I wonder how we survived it, but thank God, we did. YES, WE DID! And because we have chosen to follow God's leading, we accept that trials are inevitable in our lives, marriage, and parenting, but together, we will overcome. "He will cover you with his feathers, and under his wings you will find refuge; his faithfulness will be your shield and rampart" (Psalm 91:4).

CHARGE *to Readers:*

I challenge you to hold on to God's unchanging hand even in the toughest seasons of your life and marriage. God is faithful, and His grace is sufficient to keep you (2 Corinthians 12:9).

READER'*s action plan for today:*

Identify some of the challenges that you have faced in life or in your marriage relationship and note the impact it has had upon your overall well-being. Thank God for the ones that you have surmounted and ask Him for guidance and grace to endure and conquer the ones you're currently facing.

1. _____

2. _____

3. _____

I Wish

My Darling Courtney,

Oh, how I wish I had appreciated the beautiful changes your love and commitment had brought to my life from the very beginning. But, sometimes, we become so accustomed to the 'little' things in our lives that we fail to recognize their worth. And it is usually later that we realize that the very things that we consider so 'little' and take for granted are the things that give meaning to our life.

I know it is sometimes difficult for us to admit, but unconsciously, our upbringing defines and shapes the things we look for in our future spouses. It is probably because everything in nature comes in pairs and all of us are in search of the perfect fit. I was no exception to this rule. But I can't thank God enough for letting us find each other without even looking. I believe in the proverb "couples are made in heaven" now more than ever. Yet, there is a part of me that still wishes I could have given you my heart and loved you the way you deserved to be loved from the start.

I know wishing won't change the past, but I want you to know that if it were possible, I would do so without a second thought. So, here is to wishing...

I wish I knew what God had blessed me with from the very start. You told me you would wait for me until I was ready to commit my heart to you, knowing fully well that it would have taken quite some time. Yet, you waited, and refused to entertain the love or affection of anyone else. Oh, how I wish I saw just how special and rare you were. Oh, how I wish I could go back in time and rewrite the past.

I wish I had waited for the one who wants to show me off, the one who holds me dearly in the center of his heart.

I wish I was obedient and waited as God had instructed me to wait until marriage before giving myself away. But thank you for showing me the true meaning of "intimacy" without being "intimate." Thank you for making me feel loved without focusing on the act of making love. Thank you for reminding me that I am special and carefully crafted with love, sent especially from our Heavenly Father above.

I wish I had appreciated your commitment to always be there for me. I only saw you as another friend even though you had proven time and time again that you were committed to me 'til the very end. Thank you for always being there for me when others walked out on me. Thank you for laughing at my jokes and for making me feel special even when I was at my worse.

I love you without knowing how or when it all started.

I love you because God saw it fit to bless me with the best man He saw as my perfect fit.

I love you in this way because I do not know any other way to love you.

I pray that God will continue to bless our hearts for all eternity.

Love always,
Your wife, Sher

Personal Application

CONVICTION *from the Scriptures:*

> *Above all, love each other deeply, because love covers over a multitude of sins.* (1 Peter 4:8)

> *No eye has seen, no ear has heard, and no mind has imagined what God has prepared for those who love him.* (1 Corinthians 2:9)

> *Two are better than one, because they have a good return for their labor: If either of them falls down, one can help the other up. But pity anyone who falls and has no one to help them up. Also, if two lie down together, they will keep warm. But how can one keep warm alone?* (Ecclesiastes 4:9)

> *Let the morning bring me word of your unfailing love, for I have put my trust in you. Show me the way I should go, for to you I entrust my life.* (Psalm 143:8)

COMMITMENT *from this day forward:*

I could never imagine in my wildest dreams that God would have prepared someone as wonderful as you for me. Surely, His divine power has given us everything we need for a godly life through our knowledge of Him who called us by His own glory and goodness (2 Peter 1:3).

CHARGE *to Readers:*

Sometimes, we run ahead of God, on our own agendas, to satisfy our own selfish desires. So often, we embrace things that are not in God's perfect will for our lives. Yet God, in His great mercy, forgives us, cleanses us, and restores us through grace back to Himself. Today, learn to wait patiently upon the Lord. Align your plans with His and watch Him do amazing things that will really cause you to evaluate how you have been living your life.

READER*'s action plan for today:*

List some of the things you wish you knew before or did differently in your life as it relates to the choices you've made and that have negatively affected your marriage. Identify ways to address those issues in a loving, healthy, nonjudgmental way that enhances your life and that of your marriage.

1. _____

2. _____

3. _____

My Greatest Desire

My love,

It is my greatest desire as your wife to love you unconditionally, to love you like Christ does, always willing to sacrifice my life if that's what it takes to give you your life. But I would be lying if I didn't say there are days when I dislike your attitude and days when I even hated most of the things you did. But through it all, I NEVER ONCE STOPPED loving you.

It is my greatest desire to always treat you with the utmost respect and to honor and cherish you. But I would be lying if I didn't say there were days when I know saying the wrong word(s) at the wrong time(s) would hurt you and send you spiraling down the wrong path. But through it all, I hold your best interest dear to my heart.

It is my greatest desire to not criticize you or question your parenting skills but to let you be the BEST dad the way you know how. But I would be lying if I didn't say there are days when I want you to fail just so I can say I told you so. But through it all, your best attempt is all that I sincerely ask.

It is my greatest desire to see you spend more time studying the Word of God and meditating on His divine instructions rather than spending so much time watching your favorite TV shows. But I would be lying if I didn't say you have grown and matured a lot these past months, waking up early to pray with me and having worship with the children and even calling for worship when I forget.

It is my greatest desire to see you help around the house, help me with the dishes, take the trash out when the bin is full, and help fold the laundry once it's done. But I would be lying if I didn't say you have done it all and exceeded my expectations, and you even enjoy cooking dinner for us once in a while.

It is my greatest desire to see you put your phone down and spend more time with the kids, take them out for a walk, watch them ride their bikes, and play their favorite game of hide and seek. But I would be lying if I didn't say that you are doing just that and going above and beyond that which I ask.

It is my greatest desire to spend the rest of my life with you, to see you happy and fulfilled while we grow together in Christ and raise our children to love God and all others. But I would be lying if I didn't say that is my prayer every day and that I am excited about what the Lord has in store for the rest of our lives together.

Love always,
Your wife, Sher

Personal Application

CONVICTION *from the Scriptures:*

> *Love is patient, love is kind. It does not envy, it does not boast, it is not proud. It does not dishonor others, it is not self-seeking, it is not easily angered, it keeps no record of wrongs. Love does not delight in evil but rejoices with the truth. It always protects, always trusts, always hopes, and always perseveres. Love never fails.* (1 Corinthians 13:4–8)

> *Behold, You desire truth in the inward parts, and in the hidden part you will make me to know wisdom.* (Psalm 51:6)

> *I sought the Lord, and he answered me, he delivered me from all my fears.* (Psalm 34:4)

> *So do not fear, for I am with you; do not be dismayed, for I am your God. I will strengthen you and help you; I will uphold you with my righteous right hand.* (Isaiah 41:10)

COMMITMENT *from this day forward:*

As I continue to pray for you, Courtney, I promise to love you, cherish you, honor you, and respect you for as long as we both shall live. I am grateful every day for all you are to our family and to me. Courtney, I pray that you will continue to allow the Lord to lead and direct you as you lead our family. I pray that all your priorities will be in perfect order with those of the Lord.

CHARGE *to Readers:*

There is no greater freedom than to be at peace with God in your inner man. Therefore, accentuate the positive attributes of those within your sphere of influence instead of always pointing out the negative ones. By God's grace, strive to focus on making life better for yourself and for others in every situation. A life of misery is not a life well-lived, so purpose to be an agent of change and do it with a loving, compassionate, caring, and forgiving spirit.

READER'*s action plan for today:*

Identify ways in which your life has been blessed by your willingness to walk in love and obedience to God's instructions concerning your role as a wife, mother, and/ or person of faith especially in times when you'd rather do things your way.

1. _____

2. _____

3. _____

We Are Blessed Beyond What
We Could Have Asked For

My dear husband,

We didn't get to spend a lot of time together after our wedding day because I had to go back to school in another state. However, a few months after marriage, and yet a few months after graduation, we conceived our first child. Fate would not have it though, for after nine short weeks, we lost our precious child.

Thank you for praying with me during that difficult time. Thank you for holding me tightly when I needed to cry. Thank you for giving me the space I needed to seek God on my own, and thank you for not making me feel like it was my fault.

God, in His infinite blessing, blessed us with our miracle child, Josiah, one month after losing our first baby. He is my first love and the child that gives me reason and purpose. The love I have for him chills my spine. I didn't know I was capable of loving someone so much. He is everything we prayed for and dreamed he would be: beautiful from the crown of his head to the soles of his feet. He was the happiest baby you could ever meet, yet the baby that cried from the moment he entered this world up until now. His love is captivating and melts my heart every time. His love for me is the purest I have ever seen or experienced. We did not know it then, but he is brilliant, LOVING, determined, charming, and has the most beautiful smile. He's also the greatest little helper we could ever find. He is witty, yet shy; VERY STRONG-WILLED, but still polite. He HATES sleeping or sleeping alone and, at times, struggles with sharing and being kind, but the child I PRAYED FOR is the child I have. I cannot imagine a day without him or his love in my life.

Eighteen short months later, God blessed us again, and we conceived our second child, James. My heart melts with joy at the thought of his name. James is our light in the darkness, our peace in the storm. He is our joy when the day's woes have beaten us down, and we want to escape the realities of our failures from that day. He is the child God knew we NEEDED and blessed us with. His love overwhelmed my heart from the very first moment I held him in my arms until this day. He is the child every parent dreams of having. I cannot imagine a day without him in my life.

Thirteen months after James, we conceived our third child: a miracle baby girl. Our beautiful, unplanned "passion" baby was indeed a reward from God. We didn't know it was possible to love another human being this much even after experiencing the purest form of love twice already. We see her little personality already forming: calm, very strong-willed, loving (love giving us kisses), determined and very active, friendly and attentive but very curious and eager to play with her brothers.

I know we are blessed beyond what we could have ever asked God for, but I would be lying if I say we were prepared to parent children with totally different temperaments, personalities, idiosyncrasies, and love languages, or even remotely prepared for the amount of time and energy it would take to cater to and nurture each of their individual needs.

I must admit that this journey is a lot harder than I anticipated. We have made a lot of mistakes along the way; we had many high days, but also many low ones too. Many nights, I cried myself to sleep because I knew, for a fact, that I failed the children those days. And I would be lying if I didn't say our parenting techniques, at times, were not the best. There were times when we did not work together in disciplining or correcting the children, times when we openly rebuked each other in front of the kids, and times when we outright made a mess of everything.

I know how much I have struggled with my own obsessions with perfectionism and critical inner tape recordings, which make parenting even more difficult than I ever anticipated. I worry all the time that I am not patient enough, fun enough, loving enough, or even enough at all. I worry I am too hard on them and that I shout too much. I worry about not praying for them enough. I worry that you don't spend time with them enough. I worry about not doing the right thing by homeschooling them, and I am terrified that my behaviors will spill out on to them, perpetuating the vicious cycle I have so much tried to eradicate.

But the truth is, all my insecurities stem from what I have experienced in my childhood. I want to be the perfect mom. I also want to be the perfect wife, but thank God for reminding me that He is PERFECT, and all that I need I can and will find in Him if I trust Him and surrender all my insecurities to Him.

God gave us our children on purpose because He knew precisely what He was doing but, more importantly, what we needed. We've got this! Our calling is to reflect God's love to our children. Although we have fallen short on many occasions, and will continue to do so, I know that God has given us much more than our insecurities. He has given us EACH OTHER AND OUR CHILDREN.

Love always,
Your wife, Sher

Personal Application

CONVICTION *from the Scriptures:*

> *The Lord is my light and my salvation—whom shall I fear? The Lord is the stronghold of my life—of whom shall I be afraid?* (Psalm 27:1)

> *I have no greater joy than to hear that my children are walking in the truth.* (3 John 1:4)

> *Children's children are a crown to the aged, and parents are the pride of their children.* (Proverbs 17:6)

> *Planted in the house of the Lord, they will flourish in the courts of our God. They will still bear fruit in old age, they will stay fresh and green, proclaiming, "The Lord is upright; he is my Rock, and there is no wickedness in him."* (Psalm 92:13–15)

COMMITMENT *from this day forward:*

We are truly blessed beyond measure. We've been through so much together in molding these young lives, yet God remains faithful and gracious toward us. I am happy I have you to raise them with because, together, we are stronger as we trust in the Lord with all our hearts and lean not on our own understanding (Proverbs 3:5). As we continue to seek God's direction, I pray that we never forget His promises to deliver us from the enemies (2 Kings 17:39), protect us from evil (Proverbs 16:6), keep His eyes on us (Psalm 33:18), show us His mercy (Luke 1:50), and supply all of our needs (Psalm 34:9).

CHARGE *to Readers:*

Parenting is trial and error; there is no set manual out there that works for everyone. We each do our best to raise our children aright as God would have us do. We trust that in the process, we would get some things right. "Many things about tomorrow, I don't seem to understand, but I know who holds tomorrow, and I know who holds my hand" (Ira Standphill).

READER's *action plan for today:*

Can you count all of your blessings? Take the time to name a few of the blessings that you have received as a result of getting married, having children, or being in a position of influence at home or in a community that you're a part of. Celebrate these blessings!

1. _____

2. _____

3. _____

The Fulfillment

This section is a compilation of letters to Josiah, James, and Jade. It captures the joys and frustrations of parenthood, and looks at the blessings afforded to us as stewards in childbearing and childrearing. It's a glimpse, through the lenses of eternity, into the heart of our Heavenly Father as He demonstrates His love to us as His children. His plans are perfect, and He knows what's best for each of us.

Children are a heritage from the LORD, *an offspring and reward from him. Like arrows in the hands of a warrior are children born in one's youth. Blessed is the man whose quiver is full of them.*

—Psalm 127:3–5

Josiah

For This Child I Prayed

My darling son,

You are exactly what I asked God for—the hair on your head, the color of your eyes, your smile. It's just like mine—your analytical ability, your looks, and yes, you are beautiful, and your personality is exactly like mine. You were perfect from the moment I saw you on the ultrasound, and you still are. You were and still are everything I dreamt you would be and more.

Oh, how I love you, my strong-willed child. My mind is too finite to comprehend how it is possible for someone so stubborn, fighting at every chance you get, and throwing temper tantrums to be so loving, lovable, kindhearted, charming, and as friendly as you are.

On countless nights, I have fallen asleep exhausted from the day's battles. So many times, I have laid awake at 2:00, 3:00, or 4:00 A.M. worrying about you and that fiery temper of yours. On so many occasions, I have had to put myself in time-out for fear of doing something out of frustration that I will regret for the rest of my life.

I am so grateful that you are my firstborn and my first love because you, my child, have taught me how to love someone in spite of and not because. I cannot tell you how many nights I have fallen asleep crying, praying to God, beseeching Him to show me how to care for you, how to be patient with you, how to make sure I love you unconditionally because my greatest fear is to EVER make you feel unloved.

It might not seem like I love you because at times I discipline you but know that I really do love you.

The daily battles are endless; they leave me exhausted, heartbroken, and disappointed in myself. I question whether I am a fit mom, a good mom, and even whether I was an abusive mom because, sometimes, I had to spank you. I ask whether God made a mistake by allowing me to be your mom. The endless self-doubts and disappointment left me heartbroken. But just at the brink of giving up, I would hear the small voice, the sweetest voice I have ever heard whispering, "Mommy, I love you. Please forgive me for shouting at you today. Please hold me."

And just like that, you are in my arms, giving me the softest, gentlest, and most precious hug anyone has ever given me. In that instant, tears of joy would come streaming down my face as I softly whisper a prayer of thanksgiving to God while I gently squeeze you, holding on to you as though you are breathing your last breath and as though if I let go, you will cease to exist.

Your will is made of steel, and you have shown us that from day one. You came out crying and screaming, and you are still crying and screaming today, my son. You keep us on our toes, trying to control every outcome. but even with all the fights, you are the "best" gift I have ever received, my most precious child.

Your toddler years, oh man, I did not think I would survive. "No" was the operative word from you for EVERYTHING. It was a constant battlefield. Your nap times and bedtime routines were dreaded, and more often than not, you went to bed in tears. And so did I.

Your tantrums were epic: at the playground because it was time to go home, the grocery stores, sitting in your car seat, and at church. You threw tantrums for several reasons including: because we had to leave, because we had to turn the television off, because I wouldn't let you drown yourself, because I had to use my phone, because I wouldn't let you wear your sandals during winter, and even because the sky was blue. You have always been eager to express yourself and assert your authority on everyone.

My son, I pray continually for you and take courage in the fact that you are God's will for me (for us), in Christ Jesus (1 Thessalonians 5:16–18). You are God's gift to us, and by His grace, we will channel your strong will into meaningful ways for the glory of God. I commit to "train you up in the way you should go, that when you are older, you will not depart from it" (Proverbs 22:6).

"For this child I prayed, and the LORD has granted me what I asked of him. So now I give him to the LORD. For his whole life he will be given over to the LORD" (1 Samuel 1:27–28).

Love always,
Mom

Personal Application

CONVICTION *from the Scriptures:*

> *Children are a heritage from the Lord,*
> *offspring a reward from him. Like arrows*
> *in the hands of a warrior are children born*
> *in one's youth. Blessed is the man whose*
> *quiver is full of them.* (Psalm 127:3–5)

> *For My thoughts are not your thoughts,*
> *neither are your ways My ways, declares the*
> LORD. *For as the heavens are higher than*
> *the earth, so My ways are higher than your*
> *ways and My thoughts than your thoughts.*
> (Isaiah 55:8–9)

> *The Lord is my strength and my defense;*
> *he has become my salvation.* (Exodus 15:2)

> *There is no fear in love. But perfect love*
> *drives out fear, because fear has to do with*
> *punishment. The one who fears is not made*
> *perfect in love.* (1 John 4:18)

> *Folly is bound up in the heart of a child,*
> *but the rod of discipline will drive it far*
> *away.* (Proverbs 22:15)

COMMITMENT *from this day forward:*

There is nothing under the sun that can separate you from the love I have for you. I promise to be your biggest advocate and your loudest cheerleader. I will support all your dreams, and I will empower you, by God's grace, to accomplish them and help you reach your full potential. By God's grace and His power, I pray that all of my maladies and Daddy's will not be passed on to you. I bind every inherited woe from our generation. You will live and abide in the presence of the Lord every day of your life. Meekness, patience, and gentleness will be upon your life. The divine favor of God will abide with you, and "the LORD will watch over your coming and going both now and forevermore" (Psalm 121:8). "No weapon that is formed against thee shall prosper; and every tongue that shall rise against you in judgment thou shalt condemn" (Isaiah 54:17).

CHARGE *to Readers:*

It often feels so much easier to love and embrace the docile, acquiescent, submissive child. It is many times trying and challenging to raise a strong-willed child. Take comfort in the fact that our Heavenly Father handpicked and molded each child just for you (Psalm 139:13–14). His grace will keep you as you rely on Him to teach you how to care for this heritage that He has loaned to you (Psalm 127:3).

READER'S *action plan for today:*

List three traits you love the most in your strong-willed child or that one child that challenges your authority at every turn. Explain why you love and admire those traits the most.

1. _____

2. _____

3. _____

Mommy's Little Helper

My darling Josiah,

I sat on my bed putting your baby sister to sleep, and for a brief moment, my eyes lifted from her face, and I gazed across the room to see you sitting on the chair, playing on your phone and repeating the fifty states and their capitals to yourself. In that moment, I fell in love with you all over again. It was like the very first time I saw you, touched you, and kissed your face. How vividly I remember the first time the warmth of your body touched my chest. Oh, my child, there are simply no words to truly describe what my heart felt in that moment.

You were unaware that I was basking in your love, but reality soon kicked in and took hold of my senses as I promptly asked you to turn down the volume of your phone because it was disrupting your sister. Without hesitation you replied, "Okay, Mommy." Then you asked, "Is that okay?"

With a smile on my face and a soft reply, I said, "Yes, and thank you."

Again, I interrupted your game to ask you to get the baby's monitor for me, and again, you did as I asked without fussing or murmuring. My mind went back to the Word of God saying, "Do all things without murmurings and disputings" (Philippians 2:14). I watched you leave my room in an attempt to find the monitor but came back a few short seconds perplexed because you did not understand what I had asked you to do. I smiled because, in that moment, I saw your dad in you. I simply repeated my request, and this time, you understood. You got the monitor, plugged it in, and turned it on without me asking.

"Mommy, is that okay?" you questioned.

I replied with a proud smile on my face, "Yes, baby. It is perfect."

In that moment, I realized you were no longer a baby, but in every sense, you were and still are my baby. I see your amazing personality beginning to take shape, and I marvel at the "little" young man you are becoming. Your love and kindness are pure and unbridled, refreshing, contagious, and charming. You epitomize the very word of Scripture that the child "grew in wisdom and stature, and in favor with God and man" (Luke 2:52).

I see how much you love your brother (James) and baby sister (Jade). I see how you get upset and, sometimes, angry at us when we scold James. I see how eager you are to help me make dinner and wash the dishes. You love helping me vacuum the house even though, sometimes, you give me more work than I had before. Your favorite phrase is: "Mommy, if you are ever in need, just call for me." I love hearing you say those words; they melt my heart every time.

I have watched you change as the seasons come and go. But I want you to know that being called your mom is one of my most treasured blessings. I want you to know that I am honored that I get to share in this adventure called life with you. I want you to know that I am grateful that God has chosen me as well as found me worthy to care for you. I also want you to know that there is nothing you can do that will ever cause me to stop loving you.

I love you the most when you are mad, sad, or screaming at the top of your lungs. I love you the most when you are having just the worst day, and listening to me is the last thing you want to do. I love you because, in those moments, I want to do everything right by you. I want to teach you how to speak kind words instead of mean words. I want to teach you that there is a right and a wrong way to do everything. I want to teach you that life will have obstacles, that there are going to be times when things will not go your way, and you will have to adapt to changes. In those moments, I want to show you that I love you and that you will always be my baby, no matter what life throws at you. But more importantly, I want to show you how God treats us even when we are disobedient, and we dishonor His teachings and commandments.

I love you, my son,
Mom

Personal Application

CONVICTION *from the Scriptures:*

> *My son, hear the instruction of thy father, and forsake not the law of thy mother: For they shall be an ornament of grace unto thy head, and chains about thy neck.* (Proverbs 1:8–9)

> *If you are willing and obedient, you shall eat the good of the land; but if you refuse and rebel, you shall be devoured by the sword; for the mouth of the Lord has spoken.* (Isaiah 1:19–20)

> *My heart is confident in you, O God; my heart is confident. No wonder I can sing your praises!* (Psalm 57:7)

COMMITMENT *from this day forward:*

"Greater love hath no man than this, that a man lay down his life for his friends," (John 15:13). My life is meaningless if I cannot teach you and show you the love of God through my love for you. Nothing in this world is more important than knowing you are loved. My life I will give to protect yours if that is what it takes. I want you to know that your heart will be protected in my heart, and our home will forever be your home no matter how far life takes you from home. But above all, my darling son, I wish you will always know that I love you with every fiber in my being, yet my love cannot be compared to the love of God for you. May you continue to grow in stature before Him. "Blessed is the one who trusts in the LORD, whose confidence is in Him" (Jeremiah 17:7).

CHARGE *to Readers:*

Remember to always celebrate the small things your child(ren) does to help you around the house. I know, sometimes, in an attempt to help us, they sometimes give us more work, but I encourage you to use those opportunities to teach and instill in them the desire to learn as well as teach them proper ways to complete different tasks. I would also admonish you not to focus on the child(ren)'s lack of expertise or their deficiencies. Instead, praise them for assisting you. Also, pray that the Lord will continue to enable them to experience joy in learning and assisting you.

READER*'s action plan for today:*

List different ways you have helped your child(ren) maintain their love for helping you around the home. If not, is there anything you think you could have done differently to help nurture their love for helping? Based on the responses provided in the second section of this question, write down how you plan to put your answers into action, thereby, helping to nurture your child(ren)'s love of helping at home.

1. _____

2. _____

3. _____

My Gifted Child

My darling Josiah,

It is with a humble heart that I write you this letter. I had to in order to let you know that you are *gifted*, and it is very important that, as you grow older, you do not allow others to intimidate you or make you feel less than who God has created you to be. I do not want you to ever feel ashamed of your blessings. But if, for any reason, you are unable to elude any negative thoughts from your mind, always remember that Mommy and Daddy are your biggest advocates, and we will always support you. God has blessed you with an amazing gift, and that's the ability to recall and remember anything that you have been taught. In other words, you learn things quickly and easily. This is a blessing, and I do not want you to ever think otherwise. God has blessed you with this amazing potential, and this world is your platform to be anyone you choose to be.

I knew you were *special*; I just didn't know how special you would be. You were only a year old and barely saying a full sentence but counting from one to twenty. By your second birthday, you could say and spell your full name. You knew your two times, five times, and ten times table. You mastered counting from one to one hundred as well as counting from one hundred to a thousand. You were able to name all the colors and basic shapes. You knew our home address, Mommy's and Daddy's names, and Mommy's phone number.

I knew you were *special*; I just didn't know how special you would be. At three years old, you knew shapes I have never heard of before. You mastered the times table from two to twelve. You knew all the planets in the solar system and all the things that made them different and special. You knew how to add, multiply, and subtract mathematical problems. You memorized the road signs and make it your duty to tell us whether we are abiding by the law every time we are driving.

I knew you were *special*; I just didn't know how special you would be. At four years old, you knew all fifty states and their capitals. You could tell me all the states by looking at just their shapes. You read fluently and your favorite books to read were those with Scripture texts and Bible stories. You hated writing and, many times, cried for extended periods of time when it was time for you to do writing exercises. But you loved spelling. Some of your favorite words to spell were numbers, days of the week, and colors. You were also quick to point out whenever I made a mistake and would get very impatient whenever I was unable to remember some of the things I already taught you.

Sometimes, I would forget that you were only four years old. But my forgetfulness usually didn't last very long because you would always do something that reminded me that you are still a child. One of your favorite things to do is to throw temper tantrums and cry at the top of your lungs. It drives me insane, but I guess that's just part of your job as my child. Jumping off the sofa and climbing on the dining table is another. Oh yes, and let me not forget, writing on the wall is a classic, although you hate writing in your book and have cried every time you were told it's time for school.

Oh, my child, the thought of not being able to protect you from this world makes my heart hurt. I am sometimes filled with anxiety at the thought of you being treated differently or marginalized because you are misunderstood. I pray every day for wisdom because I want to ensure I am doing what's best for you. A great responsibility rests upon me because whatever I have taught you today, will help to mold and shape your character to become the man you will be one day. But I have hope and confidence in God to protect you all the days of your life. I pray you will use your gift to bring honor and glory to His name. I declare that "Your gift shall go before you and make room for you before great men" (Proverbs 18:16). I pray you will remain humble and not haughty. I pray you will use your talents to always help those in need.

I wrote all this down to show you that you are indeed *special*. But most importantly, I want to write you this letter because I need you to know and understand that life is what you make of it. It will not always be easy, and you will not get everything you ask for or desire, but even in the most challenging times, never forget that you have a voice and the power to change things.

I also want to give you some motherly advice for when you become a man.

- Always remember that God is your creator, sustainer, and provider; you do not accomplish anything in this life in your own strength or natural ability. Remember, you can do all things through Christ who gives you strength (Philippians 4:13). So call on God to give you strength and courage whenever you are faced with challenges in this life. He is never too busy. You might get too busy for Him, but God is never too busy for you. He is always there if you need a friend.
- Please, my child, always remember to show respect to everyone, even if you do not think they deserve to be respected. Remember, in everything, to set an example by saying and doing what is good and right. Such teaching shows integrity,

seriousness, and soundness of speech that cannot be condemned, "in that way those who oppose you may be ashamed because they have nothing bad to say" (Titus 2:7–8). Be respectful to your elders, your teachers, and your friends. I especially expect you to be respectful to your wife, when the time comes.

- It is my prayer that you will live out your potential, and in doing so, never expect others to treat you differently because Mommy or Daddy think you are special. Be willing to work hard for everything you need in this life, because diligent hands will rule, but laziness ends in forced labor (Proverbs 12:24).

- Be humble enough to say "I'm sorry" or "Please, forgive you me." Be brave enough to say "I love you!" I know this will probably be among the greatest challenges you will face, and I know this because I've been there many times, but it is those challenging moments that define true character. Remember, my darling Josiah, it is extremely important to forgive others their trespasses because only then can your Heavenly Father also forgive you (Matthew 6:14–15).

- Always remember that you have a choice no matter what the situation may be. Hence, choose wisely because every choice you make comes with its own consequences.

- Never forget those who have helped you along life's path. Write them on your heart (Proverbs 3:3). And NEVER think of yourself as better than others, regardless of your position in life. ALWAYS treat others with respect and dignity. "Don't be selfish;

don't try to impress others. Be humble, thinking of others as better than yourselves" (Philippians 2:3).

- You have told me many times that you want to be the president, and I will support and encourage your dreams, but I want you to know that success is not measured by your job, your education, how much money you possess, what kind of car you drive, or even the type of friends you have. Rather, success is determined by who you are, how you treat others, and the legacy you leave behind long after you're gone.

So whatever you choose to become, will be fine with me. If it is the President of the United States of America, as you say every day, a doctor, an astronaut, maybe a lawyer like your granddad, or even an artist, I will always be proud of you, always have been, and always will be. Remember, on all occasions, to be proud of who you are! I know your dad and I are. I love you, my gifted child.

Love always,
Mom

Personal Application

CONVICTION *from the Scriptures:*

> *Everyone who heard about it reflected on these events and asked, "What will this child turn out to be?" For the hand of the Lord was surely upon him in a special way.* (Luke 1:66)

> *As each one has received a gift, minister it to one another, as faithful stewards of God's grace in its various forms.* (1 Peter 4:10)

> *To each one of us grace was given according to the measures of Christ's gift.* (Ephesians 4:7)

> *I always thank my God for you because of his grace given you in Christ Jesus. For in him you have been enriched in every way—with all kinds of speech and with all knowledge—God thus confirming our testimony about Christ among you. Therefore you do not lack any spiritual gift as you eagerly wait for our Lord Jesus Christ to be revealed.* (1 Corinthians 1:4–7)

COMMITMENT *from this day forward:*

My darling son, please remember that Daddy and I will always be here for you no matter what the circumstances, but more importantly, I want you to never forget you are "God's gifts and his call can never be withdrawn" (Romans 11:29). He has blessed you forever, and it is your responsibility to be a good steward of His blessings on you. You are *special* not for yourself but to bless others in your generation, for the glory of our God. Josiah you are a precious trust committed to us from God, which God will one day hold us accountable for. Therefore, I am committed to educate and train you in the admonition of the Lord. There is a higher calling on your life, and as God reveals to me His plan and purpose for your life, I promise to work tirelessly to make sure you fulfill His plan and purpose.

CHARGE *to Readers:*

Showing favoritism spans all the way back to Bible history, and the Bible makes it clear that the results were devastating in Genesis 27 and Genesis 37. See to it that you do not place one child above another. I implore every parent, once God has given you a glimpse of your child's gift or talent, it is extremely important that you resist the urge to treat that child differently from his or her sibling(s). Pray and ask God to give you the wisdom and strength to discern what is right and the ways in which you should parent your child(ren). Pray continually for wisdom and understanding, always seeking God's guidance so that you keep the child on the path that leads to everlasting life. Pride will well up in the heart of the child if he or she thinks he is better than his or her sibling(s). Be diligent, watchful, and prayerful at all times.

READER's *action plan for today:*

What gifts, talents, or special abilities have you observed in your child(ren)? How can you help your child(ren) nurture and develop these gifts and talents?

1. _____

2. _____

3. _____

I Remember

My darling Josiah,

How quickly time passes, sometimes, without us even taking notice. I look at you now, and I can't believe that you are already five years old. What a wonderful journey it has been for me. I remember the day you were conceived like it was only yesterday. I remember the day I took the pregnancy test. Daddy and I stood in front of the mirror in tears. We were so excited, so careful, and so scared all at once because it was only a few weeks prior that we had "lost" your sister or brother to a miscarriage.

I remember the first time I heard your heartbeat, so faint yet so powerful. I remember the first time I saw your face on the ultrasound machine. It is still the most beautiful picture I have ever seen. I remember when I was told that you were a boy. I cried. I prayed. I danced. And then I cried some more. I remember when Daddy bought your very first outfit. I washed it, ironed it, and took maybe a dozen pictures of it. I shared it with all my friends and family. I was so excited that I was going to have a baby, and I wanted everyone to know. I remember the first time I felt the tiny flutters in my tummy and your very first kick. I remember how you kept me up all night long even before you entered this world. I should have known then that you were going to be just like your mommy.

I remember the first time I heard your very first unforgettable screams. Oh, those screams still put a smile on my face. It's like nothing I have ever heard before. They pierced my heart then, and still do today. I remember the first time you lay upon my chest. The warmth of your body chilled my spine. The soft touch of your hands stroking my face as I moved your tiny hands up and down my face is a moment that's forever etched in my memory. Your beauty was captivating. You were absolutely the most beautiful baby I had ever seen. Your long curly hair and brown eyes pierced my soul. I couldn't stop staring at you. I refused to let the nurses take you from my room unless Daddy was with you. I was overprotective of you then, and I am still overprotective of you now. I remember how scared I was to leave the hospital because I had no idea how I was going to care for this tiny human. But Daddy and I took turns sleeping, making sure you were safe, and your needs were met.

I remember watching you sleep even though I was advised to sleep when you sleep. I couldn't bear the thought of not seeing you. But truth be told, I was more afraid of something happening to you while I slept. I recorded everything you did. I took pictures of you from the moment you were awake and even while you slept. I remember the time I left you alone to use the restroom, and you aspirated on your puke. I drove 110 miles at top speed with you in my arms. The entire way to the hospital, I was praying and crying. I remember when the helicopter landed; that sound never left my memory. I watched them take you away. I couldn't breathe. My entire body was in shock, completely frozen in the same spot where they took you from my arms. I temporarily forgot how to drive or even how to put gas in my truck because of that incident. It was the scariest moment of my entire life, but I am thankful that our Heavenly Father was watching over us throughout that ordeal. That experience changed my life forever and set the course for the mom I am today. Thank you for being so strong even without knowing it. Thank you, God, for saving my most precious baby boy.

I remember the first time you crawled. I was so excited that I called your dad at work screaming. I remember your very first word—mama. That Monday morning was one of, if not my most precious moment of being a mom. I remember your first step and how you struggled to get back up after falling. But you were and still are determined to walk; within a mere few days I could proudly say you were walking. I remember the first time you walked in your shoes. Those blue-and-white sneakers are still my favorite pair of shoes. Oh, Mommy and Daddy were so proud of you, and you were so excited. We couldn't get you to take those shoes off without a fight.

I remember your first birthday and how we went overboard with the spending for your birthday party and gifts.

I remember your first day at school, how you cried, "Mommy, Mommy, please don't let me go." "Mommy, Mommy I want to go home with you." As your teacher "ripped" you from my arms, she promised to take care of you. But I could feel my heart bleeding in sorrow. I couldn't hold back the tears any longer as you continued to scream, "Mommy, Mommy, please don't leave me." "Mommy, Mommy, please don't let me go." In that moment, I realized that I really wasn't ready to let you go. As a result, the next few years, I homeschooled you on and off because I was still afraid to let you go. I remember calling your school every few hours to make sure you were okay and that all your needs were met. I remember preparing all your meals and snacks for school, making sure you ate from no one else but me. I remember how upset I got because your clothes were messy when I picked you up from school. I laugh at myself now as I recall how crazy my actions were. Sigh...

What a journey it has been. It's hard to believe that you are five years old. It feels like it was only yesterday that I found out I was pregnant with and would soon give birth to you. We have both grown and matured so much in these past five years. Our journey has had many ups and downs. But as I mature in Christ, I would not want it any other way. You are my purpose. You are like no other child I know. You are my child, my firstborn, and the one who made me a mother. You're the one who set the course for everyone to follow; the one who keeps me on my knees. You are my forever sidekick, my little angel sent from my Heavenly Father above. You are the only one who kisses me a thousand times and never gets tired.

Of all our children, you are the one who makes every hair on my arms stand up. You are the child who makes me smile and cry at the same time. You are the child who makes being a mom feel like the greatest gift to mankind, even on the toughest days. There is no one in this world to you like your mommy, and no one in this world to your mommy like you. We are fused at the core of our beings; our hearts are as one. The blood that courses through my veins runs through your heart. You are my dreams and hope. You are my past and future. You are my destiny!

I think about you, and my heart gets overwhelmed by the love I have for you. I talk about you, and I sometimes find myself getting teary-eyed. I cannot believe that someone as special and as precious as you are my child. How is it possible that I am so blessed? I have asked God many questions about being given you a thousand times. What makes me deserving of such love? What makes me deserving of such favor? In the middle of all my questioning, I simply thank Him for my most amazing gift—you. You are my baby. You are my firstborn. You are my first love. You are my everlasting gift.

Thank you for teaching me how to care and how to be compassionate. It wasn't easy, and I am still learning every day. Thank you for teaching me the true meaning of love without boundaries. Thank you for teaching me how to love without judgment. Thank you for teaching me patience—I still have a very long way to go, but thank God, the process is in motion. Thank you for teaching me how to cherish the smallest and simplest everyday moments of life. Thank you for loving me, my baby boy.

Love always,
Mom

Personal Application

CONVICTION *from the Scriptures:*

> *Whatever you ask in My name, that will I do, so that the Father may be glorified in the Son. If you ask me anything in my name, I will do it.* (John 14:13–14)

> *You did not chose Me, but I chose you and appointed you, that you should go and you should bear fruit, and your fruit should remain, so that whatever you might ask the Father in My name, He may give you.* (John 15:16)

> *The righteous man walks in his integrity; his children are blessed after him.* (Proverbs 20:7)

COMMITMENT *from this day forward:*

I love you more than mere words can express, and I will treasure each moment and opportunity that I have to show you that love from the depths of my heart as God gives me the capacity to love you. Josiah Michael Henry Thompson, you are my precious gift in more ways than you will ever know, and I pray that you will always know and experience the loving heart of God through me. I promise, with God's strength, to love, cherish, and protect you all the days of my life. Through you, I have developed a closer relationship with God and have learned of His unmerited love and favor, and I committed wholeheartedly to ensure that you experience the same love, grace, and favor through our relationship.

CHARGE *to Readers:*

Showing and telling your child how much you love and appreciate him or her should be seen as a gift. We know that God's love is ultimately the most important, however, a child will first experience God's love through his or her parent(s), so never be afraid to express your love to and for your child, privately as well as publicly. In fact, the way in which you express your love to your child will either open up or close off your child's heart to God. God's character is literally on trial based on your demonstration of love, patience, forbearance, and longsuffering during your interactions with your child, so ask God to show how to love and communicate love to your child. It is never too late to start. Be patient with yourself and your child as you both navigate the ups and downs or past failures. God will give you the strength. Just don't give up.

READER's *action plan for today:*

Are you certain your child knows and believes that you love him or her the way you say you do? What can you do differently to show your child that you do love him or her? If you are uncertain, ask God to reveal to you exactly what your child needs to feel loved, accepted, and a genuine sense of belonging.

1. _____

2. _____

3. _____

James

A Love Like No Other

My sweet James,

God has blessed me with three beautiful children, and I couldn't have asked for anything more, but with you my second child, I wanted a girl so desperately, and I believed with all my heart you would be a girl. However, upon opening the reveal letter, I found out you were a boy, and my heart sunk, but only for a brief moment because shortly after my selfishness and self-pity subsided, the Holy Spirit quickly reminded me that there are millions of women who would love to have a child (son), so I needed to be grateful. I repented and asked God to forgive me, and immediately, an unspeakable peace filled my heart.

So over the course of the next seven months, I anxiously awaited your arrival, my beautiful little baby, James Benjamin Edward Thompson. It took only one glimpse, and I was completely in love. Your calm disposition was alluring, and everyone who worked with you at the hospital was in awe of you. Even as a babe, your personality shone bright like the morning star. I was in awe of God's grace. He gave me what He knew I needed because He knows what it will take to save me.

I didn't think or know it was possible to love someone as much as I love you, James. Your loving personality, charming sense of humor, and outgoing personality is contagious and heartwarming. You are also independent, intelligent, a little witty, and just my little fluffy bear. You are kind and caring. You are compassionate and hate to see others sad. You are helpful and somewhat neat; you still have a lot more learning to do. But you hate to see doors and drawers open, just like your mommy! You are outgoing and friendly, charming and charismatic. You desire to see everyone happy. This is evident in your constant inquiries to know if Mommy, Daddy, Josiah, or Jade are okay. It is also evident in your constant reminders of your love for us.

I cannot, for a moment, imagine my life without you. Today, I want to remind the world that God knows what we need before we ask, and He is faithful to supply all of our needs according to His riches in glory in Christ Jesus… Amen!

My darling son, your arrival established purpose in me. You have set me to walk in the rhythm of my life and in alignment with our Heavenly Father. For He knows the plans He has for us (Jeremiah 29:11), and you are very much a part of that plan for me and our family. You are my reward from God (Psalm 127:3). James, may you always walk before the Lord, and may you and generations after you—your children, and their children after them—fear the Lord your God as long as you live (Deuteronomy 6:2).

Love always,
Mom

Personal Application

CONVICTION *from the Scriptures:*

> *Trust in the* LORD *with all thine heart; and lean not unto thine own understanding. In all thy ways acknowledge him, and he shall direct thy paths.* (Proverbs 3:5–6)

> *Be anxious for nothing, but in everything by prayer and supplication, with thanksgiving, let your requests be made known to God; and the peace of God, which surpasses all understanding, will guard your hearts and minds through Christ Jesus.* (Philippians 4:6–7)

> *You will show me the path of life; In Your presence is* fullness *of joy; At Your right hand are* pleasures forevermore. (Psalm 16:11)

> *Give thanks in all circumstances; for this is God's will for you in Christ Jesus.* (1 Thessalonians 5:18)

COMMITMENT *from this day forward:*

My darling James, it is my greatest honor to care for you and to love you. In the same respect, I promise to pay close attention to exactly who you are and who you want to be, never forcing my will or desires upon you. I promise to work hard and to put my preconceived notions about motherhood and raising "perfect" children aside so that I can see things from your perspective and direct and support you according to the instructions of God. I am committed to learning how to be patient, encouraging, and nurturing so that I can be the best mom to you, but most importantly, I am committed to teaching you the greatest love of all—God's love.

CHARGE *to Readers:*

Trust that God knows what is best for you. He will give you all that is needed for you to be successful on this earth. If you allow Him to lead and direct your path, even after you have doubted (He understands our weaknesses), you will, most assuredly, live a more peaceful life.

READER'*s action plan for today:*

Give an example of when you were disappointed about a situation concerning your child because you thought God did not give you the desire(s) of your heart. How did you handle the outcome? How did you respond when you realized that God's plan was indeed the best solution for your situation?

1. _____

2. _____

3. _____

At First Sight

My sweet baby,

The silence rang loudly in my ears; it was a melody I had never heard before. The tune was soft and captivating, and I fell in-love with your silence. Before your skin touched mine, I just knew there was an unspoken love between us like no other. I knew God had sent me a blessing, perfectly wrapped in your love, for this and every day. I thank Him.

As I sat in the dark rocking you back and forth, hoping to never let you go, you snuggled close to my heart, the place you first heard my thoughts. I wondered who will one day captivate your heart, but then I realized, your heart was already mine. So, I pulled you in closer, making sure you felt protected, safe, and warm. Your words, though unspoken, were very loud as you drew near to the place you once called your home.

Your tiny body snuggled up against mine, then you stretched and groaned as you searched frantically for my breast. At last, you found it! You latched on to it; your pulls were rhythmic, drawing in my milk, sweet and warm to your taste, so evident as you wiggled and twisted your body. Oh, my baby, how I cherish these moments of unspoken love between us, knowing they are fleeting.

During this shared moment of silence, an unbroken bond was forged and sealed for eternity, never to be broken. A foundation of love and trust was built, never to be shaken. An attitude of thankfulness was created, never to be mistaken. There is a love between us which no pain can ever erase; a love which no distance can break. This was the moment I waited for, when all my desires were abolished, and all my hidden wishes fulfilled and in full view. And as I held you close, the plentitude of your love filled my heart. It is finished! You are my true love. THIS IS THE LOVE BETWEEN YOU AND ME.

You have blessed my womb; you have blessed my heart. All my vital organs come alive especially because you are here. It is in this love that I completely understood the true meaning of the words of our Lord Jesus, "Greater love has no one than this: to lay down one's life for one's friends" (John 15:13). I love you with all my heart!

Love always and forever,
Mom

Personal Application

CONVICTION *from the Scriptures:*

> *I have loved you with an everlasting love;*
> *I have drawn you with unfailing kindness.*
> (Jeremiah 31:3)

> *And now these three remain: faith, hope*
> *and love. But the greatest of these is love.*
> (1 Corinthians 13:13)

> *I have no greater joy than to hear that my*
> *children walk in truth.* (3 John 1:4)

COMMITMENT *from this day forward:*

Courtney, as parents, we are truly blessed beyond measure. We've been through so much together in molding these young lives, yet God remains faithful and gracious toward us. I am happy I have you to raise them with because, together, we are stronger as we trust in the Lord with all our hearts and lean not on our own understanding (Proverbs 3:5). James, I pray that you will learn to trust God in all areas of your life based on the life we live and the examples we set before you. I pray that you will also grow to trust us with your heart, knowing that we will forever protect you to the best of our abilities based on the strength God has given unto us. And although I may fail some days, I promise to honor God by fulfilling His instruction to teach you His commandments while we sit at home, when we walk along the road, when we lie down, and when we get up (Deuteronomy 6:6–7).

CHARGE *to Readers:*

Relish the moments you have now with your little ones because before you know it, they will be all grown-up. Allow nothing in your life to prevent you from spending quality time with your child. You will regret it if you do not make the sacrifice now and put it off for later; by then, it will be too late. Time is no respecter of persons, and it waits for no one. Do not "love" your child based on your temporary emotional feelings. Be consistent in your display of affection, even when you are angry. Think about God's love for you; it never changes even when you disobey Him. That's the love you need to have for your child(ren).

READER's *action plan for today:*

List some unique, new, practical, and memorable ways in which you can demonstrate love to your child(ren).

1. _____

2. _____

3. _____

God Knows Our Needs before We Ask

My sweet James,

I remember meeting you for the first time, and even though you don't remember that moment, I am sure you felt that unexplainable love between us; it was strong and indescribable. As I gazed into your little brown eyes, and you into mine, in that moment, we had a conversation that required no words. You knew you were safe, and I promised to keep you safe always. You were everything I dreamed you would be—calm and unassuming, beautiful, and a blessing.

I have watched you grow, and I cannot help but wonder what the future holds for you. Who will you become? I watched your tiny hands hold on to my face for dear life, drawing me near. Whose hands will they hold on to someday? Whose finger will they slide a shiny ring upon? Your sweet kisses pierced my heart. Who will those lips kiss good night? Your tiny arms wrapped so tightly around mine. Who will someday feel their gentle embrace?

I have watched you learn to smile, hold your head up, roll over, crawl, and walk along the couch. You are my scheduled baby, in that, you sleep at the same time every day and night. You are a joy to care for and to be around. Each time I hold you in my arms, my heart is overwhelmed to the point of tears. How is it possible to experience such joy and peace in one tiny little person all at once?

I cannot wait to see how your relationship will flourish with your brother and sister, Josiah and Jade, as the three of you grow. I see the relationship between you and your dad growing into something beautiful, and I love that he loves you so unconditionally. But I thank the Lord that you still love to snuggle, and when you need Mommy, you come running. Those are the moments I cling to the most. I truly cherish those moments because I know they are fleeting as my baby boy becomes a man, and I face the reality that, one day, you will love another.

I thank God every day for giving you to me. I call you my little "Holy Spirit" because of your calm disposition, and I believe with my heart that God placed you in all our lives, but especially mine, to be a testimony of undeserved love. Through you, I understand God's love for His children. Words just aren't enough to express how grateful and blessed I am to have a son like you.

So to the woman who will someday hold the hands I have held and kiss the lips I have fed, I want you to know that I have done my best to raise a son who will treat you with respect and love you the best. I pray that he will place you above all else, with a love that knows no bounds, especially with the love of a mother's heart because, I assure you, there is no greater kind known and understood by the human mind.

Love always,
Mom

Personal Application

CONVICTION *from the Scriptures:*

> *Every good and perfect gift is from above,*
> *coming down from the Father of the*
> *heavenly lights, who does not change like*
> *shifting shadows.* (James 1:17)

> *The Lord will perfect that which concerns*
> *me; Your mercy, O Lord, endures forever;*
> *Do not forsake the works of Your hands.*
> (Psalm 138:8)

> *Your unfailing love is better than life itself;*
> *how I praise you!* (Psalm 63:3)

COMMITMENT *from this day forward:*

God has entrusted you to me, and it is my daily prayer that I will endeavor to teach you that the fear of the Lord is the beginning of wisdom; all who follow his precepts have good understanding (Psalm 111:10), but also, that fools despise wisdom and instruction (Psalm 1:7). With God's strength and my commitment to Him and you, I promise to make our home a place of love, a place where the angels of God can abide, and a place where you can laugh, be yourself, and speak freely, where you know you will be heard and where you can find rest as well as get a healthy meal. I promise to invest my time and resources in ensuring that you are loved, feel loved, and know that you are loved.

CHARGE *to Readers:*

It is so liberating to love the seed and offspring of your womb. It is also a fact that every day circumstances may sometimes make you feel otherwise. I pray that you will always know that God specially chose you to bear, raise, and give back to Him this beautiful child He has blessed you with. May you always find the strength to completely love your child as God's gift to you.

READER'*s action plan for today:*

What influences or obstacles in your life are keeping you from giving your child(ren) the love and attention that they need?

1. _____

2. _____

3. _____

Jade

My Journey to Meeting You

My beautiful baby girl,

I loved you before you were conceived. I loved you before meeting you. You ask me, "How?" Because I dreamed of you and what my life would be like if I had you. I loved you without touching or feeling your body against mine. I secretly anticipated your arrival, not knowing that my dreams would someday become a reality. And I love you even more now that you are a part of my "soul."

I called your dad straight away. He was at work. He answered the same way he does every day.

"Hey, Sher, what's up?"

"Well," with a long pause, "I think we are pregnant because yesterday was my most fertile day."

A deafening silence clogged the line between us.

As the expected shock wore off, your dad said, "We cannot afford another baby right now."

"I know, but what are we going to do?" I asked.

"We just bought a house, and you lost your job," he said.

"I know. But what are we going to do if I am pregnant? Maybe I could get another job."

"Yeah, right! Sure. I know you too well."

"I know the timing isn't ideal by our standards, but God's timing is perfect."

The silence lingered.

The conversation ended with his final words: "I am at work. We can talk about it later."

The weeks went by slowly, and the silence grew louder. Nothing was said of the imminent possibility of being pregnant. But secretly, I couldn't wait for October 30, the day I would confirm what I already knew—that I was pregnant. Nonetheless, I did the test, and I must say, it was one of the happiest days of my life but also one of the most nerve-wracking as two bright-pink lines on the pregnancy stick stared back at me. I am going to be a mom again, three times over! Thank you, God, for answering my prayers.

Now I couldn't wait to meet you. But everything about you made me nervous. I had to wait twenty weeks before knowing your sex. I was told there was a possibility of you having Down syndrome because of my age. I couldn't wait for that claim to be debunked. During those twenty weeks, I was anxious, nervous, tired, impatient, and excited all at once. I wanted you to be a girl. I just needed to know. So while I waited, I daydreamed of who you would look like. I wanted you to look like Josiah. I wanted you to be calm like James. I wanted you to have my smile. And I wanted you to be smart like your dad. I created the perfect little image of you in my head. And I must say, God gave me EXACTLY what I prayed for. You are all that I prayed for and so much more.

It was a Sabbath afternoon, February 10, 2018, to be exact. We all gathered at our home in North Carolina to find out your gender. As we prepared to pop the balloons, I could hear my heart beating in my head above all the chatter and excitement. It felt like my wedding day all over again. I laughed nervously but did the best I could to remain calm. We did the countdown…3, 2, 1, and the balloons were popped. The screams echoed loud in my head because my eyes were tightly closed, "It IS a girl!" The joy I felt in that moment was indescribable. I joined in the screams, and I jumped for joy. But I think a part of me was still in disbelief because I didn't cry. I couldn't cry. The tears just wouldn't come. The love, joy, and support in the room were pure, and my heart was filled with thanksgiving.

But once the excitement was over and everyone left, I couldn't hold the tears back. I cried uncontrollably. Could it really be true? Am I really going to have my little girl? I refused to let myself believe because I didn't see the ultrasound. The business that prepared the surprise balloons lost my ultrasound. But for the next forty-eight hours, I was merely running on adrenaline because I couldn't sleep. I couldn't wait to call my doctor's office to confirm what I already knew. Again, you were confirmed. You were a girl!

I just kept telling God, "Thank you! Thank you for answering my prayers. Thank you for trusting me with her heart." That week, I also received great news. I found out that you were a healthy baby with no signs of Down syndrome. Again, God answered my prayers.

I spent the next eighteen weeks daydreaming about meeting you. The process leading up to your delivery felt like a lifetime, but I guess, you were just as eager to meet me as I was to meet you because you came two weeks earlier than your expected arrival date. The trip to the hospital was somewhat relaxing as Mommy, Daddy, and your brothers talked about meeting you. The hours went by slowly, and you showed no signs of coming soon. So Mommy took matters into her own hands. I spent the next eighteen hours walking up and down the hospital floor with the IV that had been placed in my vein earlier. The nurses and staff watched me all night. They thought I was crazy. I exercised and did squats every hour. I talked to you, and I prayed for you. But you were determined to stay in "cozy" land.

As I neared the twenty-four-hour mark without you in sight, I was told I needed to make a decision whether to have the Pitocin (a medicine to help speed up labor), or my doctor would make the final decision. I complied after talking with some of my most trusted friends and Daddy. Your life and safety were more important than my delivery protocols.

I can't say that it was fun. The pain I experienced was ten times more excruciating than my previous births. There were moments I thought I would lose my mind. There were moments I was so frantic and screaming at the top of lungs that my doctor suggested that I take some medication to help alleviate my pain. I did not. There were moments I was lying on the floor while punching the wall because the cold floor felt better than my warm bed. There were moments I thought I would break Daddy's hand, but thank God, I didn't!

With God's help, Daddy by my side, and the amazing help of my nurses and doctor, you were placed in my arms. And just like that, I completely forgot that only a few moments before, I was about to lose my mind. The pain was replaced with tears of joy and shared excitement. And then I heard you crying. It was the perfect pitch. In any crowded room, I can identify the sound. Yours is a cry that will awaken me in the middle of the night to come sooth and rock you back to sleep. It thrilled my heart to know that, someday, the voice producing that cry would call me Mom.

This tiny being, perfect in every way, half of me and half of Daddy, was placed on my chest. And for a brief moment, between a glance and our first kiss, the world stopped. With tears in my eyes, the only words I could echo were, "What took you so long?"

This was the moment I waited for all my life. The moment I got to hold you. The moment I got to kiss you and to feel your tiny fingers clasping mine. Equally valuable was the moment I got to care for you and protect you. I could tell you knew you were safe because you stopped crying the moment you were placed on my chest. And in that moment, I thanked God. Love found me once again, and I fell in love all over again.

Love forever,
Mom

Personal Application

CONVICTION *from the Scriptures:*

Before I formed you in the womb I knew you, before you were born I set you apart. (Jeremiah 1:5)

Yet you brought me out of the womb; you made me trust in you, even at my mother's breast. From birth I was cast on you; from my mother's womb you have been my God. (Psalm 22:9–10)

For you created my inmost being; you knit me together in my mother's womb. I praise you because I am fearfully and wonderfully made; your works are wonderful, I know that full well. (Psalm 139:13–14)

Every good and perfect gift is from above, coming down from the Father of the heavenly lights, who does not change like shifting shadows. (James 1:17)

My grace is sufficient for you, for my power is made perfect in weakness. Therefore I will boast all the more gladly about my weakness, so that Christ's power may rest on me. That is why, for Christ's sake, I delight in weaknesses, in insults, in hardships, in persecutions, in difficulties. For when I am weak, then I am strong. (2 Corinthians 12:8–10)

COMMITMENT *from this day forward:*

Before you were conceived, I had been praying for you, so it is no surprise that when I found out I was pregnant with you, I prayed for you (almost) every night—even while you were in my womb. I was committed then, and I am still committed today, and until I take my last breath, I will follow the instructions of the Lord as they pertain to teaching you His commandments, precepts, and instructions.

It's important that you understand that you are not just another child. You are my daughter, given to me by God to train and mold for His consecrated purpose. So it is with joy that I commit myself to being the best mother to you. I won't pretend to know or have the answers to everything you will need to know, but I know that God does. Therefore, I promise to rely on Him for wisdom to teach and train you to be the best you can be. And as I endeavor to give you the best life, I know that God will give me the strength I need to fulfill His purpose in your life.

It is also my commitment to you to daily appeal to the throne of God for understanding so that I may teach you the importance of trusting God in all areas of your life, sacrifice, self-love and respect, sexual purity, faithfulness, love for others, humility, honesty, trustworthiness, loyalty, commitment, self-discipline and, most importantly, forgiveness—both offering and accepting this wonderful gift. The Lord promised that His grace is sufficient, and His power is made perfect in weakness (2 Corinthians 12:9), so as I tackle each day, I promise to hold fast to His words as I teach you His wisdom and statutes.

CHARGE *to Readers:*

Sometimes, we find ourselves in the hard places of life where it seems like we experience nothing but difficulty and uncertainty. I want to remind you that in spite of what we go through, God is faithful. His ways and His thoughts are higher than ours, so trust His heart in the toughest seasons of your life. He knows the plans He has for us, and they are plans to prosper and not harm us.

READER*'s action plan for today:*

What are some of the promises you have made to God about the child(ren) you have been blessed with? Have you been faithful to your vows, and if so, what has been the outcome of your faithfulness?

1. _____

2. _____

3. _____

Where Did the Time Go?

My sweet Jade,

I can't believe you are one year old already. It feels like, only yesterday, I was in the hospital awaiting your arrival. But as I celebrate each of your momentous milestones, I secretly wish I could stop the time just long enough to enjoy this stage of your life a little longer. But since time waits for no one, I will continue to relish these moments that I know are fleeting.

As the days quickly become weeks, and the weeks turn into months, I can unequivocally say these last few months have been the most transformational and exhilarating time of my life. My world, as I dreamed that it would be, is complete. God has granted me all the desires of my heart. I am left wanting nothing.

But I would be lying if I didn't say I am overwhelmed with both gratitude and fear. I am thankful for everything God has blessed me with. I am thankful that you are healthy. I am thankful that you are my beautiful baby girl. But sometimes, I am fearful of the possibility of not seeing you grow up. You see, I lost my mom at an early age, and this fear is crippling when I think of the possibility of that happening to you. I am fearful I might disappoint God and you. I am fearful of making the wrong decisions about your future. But as I sit here listing my fears, I was suddenly reminded that "God has not given us the spirit of fear; but of power, and of love, and of a sound mind" (2 Timothy 1:7). Then I breathed a sigh of relief and reminded myself "don't worry about anything; instead, pray about everything" (Philippians 4:6).

I know that, right now, you do not understand what I am saying, but when you're old enough, you will understand how important you are to me. You have given me so much joy and brighten up my days with your smiles and laughter. Every morning, I look at you, you remind me of how blessed I am to have you. You are my little angel without wings. You are my sunshine that takes the gray clouds away. I know God loves me because He gave me you. I look forward to the day I will be your best friend.

There are not enough hours in the day for me to spend with you as my time is divided between Daddy, your brothers, and the daily household chores. But by no means are you neglected. Mommy just desires to spend more time with you. I miss you when you are asleep and look forward to when you are awake. Your crib is right next to my bed, but I refuse to let you sleep alone. And even though I am tired from only getting three to five hours of sleep every night, I cherish these sleepless nights because I get to spend them uninterrupted with you. I sometimes lay next to you, anticipating your soft touch or your warm body moving up against mine. Your baby scent warms my heart as I hold you tightly and press soft kisses along your cheeks and neck. You giggle and stroke my face with your tiny hands, and I often find myself with tears in my eyes. What I love the most about waking up next to you is how calm you are. You lay next to me, humming and playing with your toy. And I get to hold you and cuddle with you just a little longer. Oh, my sweet baby girl, I will miss these precious moments. But for now, I will bask in them.

How is it that such a small person can make someone fall so madly in-love? How can such a small person fill your heart with so much joy? Your love is pure and exudes all that epitomizes the true definition of Christlikeness. I know you know you are loved, and I can tell you love me too, even though you cannot verbalize it. I see how you look at me and how you love holding my face when you kiss me. I hear how you cry when I walk into the house after being gone for an hour or two. I acknowledge how you smile at me across the room like there is no one else in the world but me.

You are growing up too quickly. Where did the time go? As I comb my fingers through your hair and gaze into your beautiful brown eyes, you smile back at me. You are already crawling, pulling yourself up, saying "Mama" and "Dada," and crying whenever you do not get things your way. It's amazing how you know exactly what you want, and if you do not get it, you will not stop crying. For example, when you are very tired and want me to stand up and walk around the room with you instead of sitting on the bed or on the chair. Sometimes, I am exhausted and just want to sit down, but you refuse to stop crying, and the moment I stand up, you stop crying as though just seconds ago you weren't screaming at the top of your lungs. But you are usually correct because you often fall asleep immediately. Then there are those moments when I am singing to you, and I can tell that you want me to stop, and if I don't, you won't stop crying. However, the moment I stop singing, you stop crying. So that you're aware, your brothers loved when I sang for them, and they still do.

I have observed how frustrated you get because you are unable to figure out how to get the light on the baby monitor or how to stop your toys from rolling away. I have also noticed how your determination encourages you not to give up until you have accomplished what you set out to do. The sheer delight in your victory is often heartwarming. I marvel at how such a small person can be so determined. This, I recognize, is a shared quality I have also seen in your brothers.

I saw how much you craved for your independence. No longer do you want me to hold you after feeding you in the nights, and I also saw your struggles too. You are not able to burp quite yet on your own, and usually, after a few seconds, you find your way back into my arms. And gladly, I would scoop you up, knowing very well what would happen. Believe me, I hated the thought of putting you down in the first place.

I know I have said it time and time again, but I love you! While you are not able to comprehend what I am saying just yet, I want you to know that no matter where life takes you, no matter what disappointments life throws at you, no matter how many times you might fail and have to start over, no matter what you do wrong, nothing can separate you from the love I have for you. It is immeasurable. And I say this without any doubt; I will always be there to catch you, if you fall. Always remember, YOU ARE BEAUTIFUL, JUST AS YOU ARE, and God loves you. I promise you that you will forever be my "angel," baby girl.

Love always,
Mom

Personal Application

CONVICTION *from the Scriptures:*

> *I thank my God for you every time I think of you; and every time I pray for you all, I pray with joy.* (Philippians 1:3–4)

> *My heart is overflowing with a good theme...Grace is poured upon your lips; therefore God has blessed you forever.* (Psalm 45:1–2)

> *I have set the Lord always before me. Because he is at my right hand, I will not be shaken. You have made known to me the path of life; you will fill me with joy in your presence, with eternal pleasures at your right hand.* (Psalm 16:8–11)

> *The Lord is righteous in all his ways and loving toward all he has made. The Lord is near to all who call on him. To all who call on him in truth.* (Psalm 145:17–18)

COMMITMENT *from this day forward:*

Giving birth to two princes came with its own set of challenges. However, giving birth to a princess has taken motherhood to a whole new level. Because of the experiences that I had in childhood and in adolescence, I have conscientiously made a commitment to set the right example for you as well as teach you how to be God-fearing and respectful of yourself and of others. I realize that time is a fleeting commodity, so instead of living with any regrets, I endeavor to value each moment we have together. By God's grace, I also resolve to make every effort to spend quality time with you each and every day, nurturing you and loving you as you deserve because my heart's desire is to give you the opportunity to grow, learn, and develop a character that will prepare you to be a beacon of light in the world around you and also prepare you for Heaven.

CHARGE *to Readers:*

The precious child you hold in your arms will one day be grown and independent and refuse to be held. Enjoy and savor every moment that you get to have and hold your baby. That child is a special gift loaned (Psalm 127:3) to you from God. It is your responsibility to care and nurture and return the child to God for His glory.

READER*'s action plan for today:*

Endeavor to spend more quality time with your children by identifying spiritual, wellness, and household activities that you can do with your child. Use these moments as opportunities to teach life skills that will sustain them as they grow and mature in their understanding of relationships with others and with their Creator.

1. _____

2. _____

3. _____

Future In-Laws

This section focuses on the priceless worth of my beautiful, precious gems, Josiah, James, and Jade. Undoubtedly, they deserve nothing less than God's absolute best and our ideal for them in a virtuous, honorable, caring, God-fearing spouse, who not only loves and respects them and their family, but more importantly, who loves the Lord with all their hearts.

*May the God of endurance and encouragement
grant you to live in such harmony with one another, in
accord with Christ Jesus, that together you may with one
voice glorify the God and Father of our Lord Jesus Christ.*

—Romans 15:5-6

To My Daughter's Future Husband

My dear future son-in-law,

It is hard to believe that today, Courtney and I give you our sweet baby girl's hand in marriage. But it gives me great joy and pride to write you this letter. Because I know God, I know that He knitted you in your mother's womb just for my baby, Jade. Therefore, I take confidence in knowing that she has chosen the man God wanted her to marry. I am delighted at the thought of giving you her hand in marriage, even though it is the most difficult thing I will ever do. I have prayed consistently for you and your parents.

I have prayed that they have taught you how to love the Lord above everything and everyone else. I have prayed that they have taught you how to be respectful and treat others with love and dignity. I have prayed that they have taught you how to be faithful—faithful to God in your tithes and offerings, faithful to God with your time and talent, faithful to your wife and your marriage. We are living in a time when sexuality is perverted, and sex and nakedness are the norm and are lurking right at our doorsteps. "Marriage should be honored by all, and the marriage bed kept pure, for God will judge the adulterer and all the sexually immoral" (Hebrews 13:4).

I have prayed that you will be a man of great self-control and discernment, knowing when and how to close the door to the enemy's traps. I have prayed that your parents have taught you that marriage is a covenant between you, your wife, and God—a covenant put in place to glorify God. Marriage is not a fairy tale. There will be difficult seasons, difficult issues that the both of you will have to discuss and pray through to resolve. There will be seasons of loss and hurt, unexpected health issues, and financial challenges.

There might even be days when you will ask yourself, "Where is my wife?" "Where is the woman I married?" But it is during those days and seasons that your faith will have to be the strongest. It is during those days and seasons that God will have to be your anchor. It is during those days and seasons that you will have to love your wife the most, fight for your marriage the hardest, and stay on your knees the longest.

Marriage is not a fairy tale. It requires love to keep it growing, prayer to keep it undergirded, and God to sustain it. I have prayed that your parents have taught you that communication and trust is the cornerstone of every successful marriage. I have prayed that they have taught you that it is okay to help your wife with the laundry, clean up the house if she is tired, take the trash out, wash the dishes once in a while, cook a meal or two every now and again, and take the children out for a ride or to have fun at the park.

I know my list might appear daunting, and I am sorry, but I need you to understand that by marrying my daughter, you are being commissioned by God to the highest and most important role of your life. "Therefore shall a man leave his father and his mother, and shall cleave unto his wife: and they shall be one flesh" (Genesis 2:24). I need to know that you understand that by marrying my daughter, you are to love her as though she is your own body.

Protect her the same way you would protect your mother. Provide for her financially. Be there for her emotionally and make a vow that you will not be physically, emotionally, or verbally abusive to her. God instructs, "Husbands, love your wives, just as Christ loved the Church and gave himself up for her" (Ephesians 5:25). I need to know that you will be the leader of your home while allowing God to guide and sustain you.

I am not looking for you to be perfect because Jade is not. However, please understand that by giving you my daughter's hand in marriage and entrusting you with her heart, this is the most difficult thing I will ever do as a parent. It is like I am giving you a part of my soul. Jade is my most treasured gift. I love her like no other. She is my baby, the child I prayed for from my youth, and raising her was my greatest joy. So giving her away to you and entrusting her to your leadership is not easy. That said, I ask of you this one thing: please protect her heart in your heart.

It is my hope that you and your parents are also praying for your future wife. But in the meantime, please know that I will raise her and teach her to honor and respect you as the leader of your home. I have taught her that marriage is not "fifty-fifty" but giving 100 percent of yourself. I have taught her the importance of commitment and loving her spouse wholeheartedly with a willingness to fight for her marriage and family during times of difficulty. I have taught her that marriage is a binding covenant, and it should be treated as such, allowing NO ONE, including her parents, to dictate the affairs of her family and household. I have taught her the importance of praying for her husband and children. I have taught her to never lose sight of who she is, to be a woman of prayer, courage, and poise, one who will respectfully voice her opinions without belittling others. I have taught her to never take your sacrifice for granted or as a sign of weakness. I have also taught her the importance of being your biggest supporter and the person you will always want to share your dreams, fears, and aspirations with. But most importantly, I have taught her the importance of saying, "I am sorry" and "I forgive you."

Your future mother-in-law,
Sher

P.S. I have prayed that your life together will be filled with love, peace, contentment, and laughter. May you both always be friends and never stop being lovers.

Personal Application

CONVICTION *from the Scriptures:*

> *Two are better than one, because they have*
> *a good return for their labor: If either of*
> *them falls down, one can help the other up.*
> *But pity anyone who falls and has no one to*
> *help them up.* (Ecclesiastes 4:9–10)

> *If two lie down together, they will keep*
> *warm. But how can one keep warm alone?*
> (Ecclesiastes 4:11)

> *To the married I give this command (not*
> *I, but the Lord): A wife must not separate*
> *from her husband. But if she does, she must*
> *remain unmarried or else be reconciled*
> *to her husband. And a husband must not*
> *divorce his wife.* (1 Corinthians 7:10–11)

COMMITMENT *from this day forward:*

I promise to be truthful and impartial on all issues that are brought before me with God's help. I promise to do my best to support you, your marriage, and the decisions you make. I promise to respect the boundaries of your marriage and not be intrusive. I promise to pray without ceasing for your union. I promise to be there for you whenever my service is requested and to respect your privacy and space.

CHARGE *to Readers:*

Fellow parents, as we entrust our child(ren) to their future and their new endeavors, we have one solid guarantee to "Train up a child in the way he should go: and when he is old, he will not depart from it" (Proverbs 22:6).

READER's *action plan for today:*

How has your life been affected by family or friends not respecting your decisions or the boundaries of your marriage? If anger, bitterness, and isolation have occurred as a result of such behavior, how can you address the situation in a peaceful manner to promote healing and restoration? What steps can you take to avoid doing the same thing to your own children when they come of age and are on their own, making decisions regarding marriage, etc.?

1. _____

2. _____

3. _____

To My Son's Future Wife[1]

My dear future daughter-in-law,

Pastor Charles Stanley once wrote to his daughter Karen, on the eve of her marriage, that "marriage is not so much finding the right person as being the right person." As parents, Courtney and I can only hope and pray for the best for our children. We trust that we have trained them up in the way that they should go and hope that when they get older, they will not depart from it (Proverbs 22:6). My son has chosen you, as you have chosen him. I love him with all my heart, and I have raised him the best way I knew. I can only hold to the promises of God to me that he will be the man he ought to be.

It is my prayer that as the head of his family, he will lead you, his wife, and the offspring produced from your union, in the right way. Further, it is my hope that as priest of his family, he will lead you before the altar of the Lord; that he will lead, as promoter, to love you as Christ loves the church and gave Himself for it; that as protector, you will never feel afraid, insecure, or unsafe; that as provider, you will never suffer lack in your basic essentials of life.

In like manner, I pray that you will honor him as your head and submit to him as he submits to the Lord. I pray that, together, you will each live for the other and for the Lord. I pray that like the Proverbs 31 woman, she will praise you in the gates and that your children will rise up and call you blessed. I pray that you will possess the tenacity, resilience, wisdom, and entrepreneurial skills of this woman to manage the financial resources of your family.

---

[1] I have two sons, so this letter is addressed to both future daughters-in-law.

Precious daughter-in-law, I have endeavored to raise a God-fearing, honorable, honest, trustworthy, faithful, hardworking, and dedicated man, according to the Word of God. My hope is that you were raised to understand the depth of this Word and to value these morals. I have prayed for you since my son was but an infant. I pray that this is truly the Lord's doing and that it is marvelous in His eyes (Psalm 118:23).

Your future mother,
Sher

P.S. I am praying that your life together will be filled with love, peace, contentment, and laughter. May you both always be friends and never stop being lovers.

Personal Application

CONVICTION *from the Scriptures:*

> *And this is the second thing you do: You cover the altar of the Lord with tears, with weeping and crying; So He does not regard the offering anymore, nor receive it with goodwill from your hands. Yet you say, "For what reason?" Because the Lord has been witness between you and the wife of your youth, with whom you have dealt treacherously; yet she is your companion and your wife by covenant. But did He not make them one, having a remnant of the Spirit? And why one? He seeks godly offspring. Therefore take heed to your spirit, and let none deal treacherously with the wife of his youth. For the Lord God of Israel says that He hates divorce, for it covers one's garment with violence, says the Lord of hosts. Therefore take heed to your spirit, that you do not deal treacherously.* (Malachi 2:13–16)

> *Marriage is honorable among all, and the bed undefiled; but fornicators and adulterers God will judge.* (Hebrews 13:4)

> *But from the beginning of the creation, God "made them male and female." For this reason a man shall leave his father and mother and be joined to his wife, and the*

> two shall become one flesh; so then they
> are no longer two, but one flesh. Therefore
> what God has joined together, let not man
> separate. (Mark 10:6–9)

COMMITMENT *from this day forward:*

Even now as children, I, on some days, struggle to let you both go. So in advance, I have begun praying and asking God to give me the strength to accept that when you both become men and husbands, I will freely and willingly relinquish my authority to influence your lives, the choices you make, and the directions of your family and to fully accept that you are now adults, and you have the authority over your own lives and homes. I promise to support and respect your personal lives and marriages and the boundaries you and your wives will have in your homes. I promise to never speak ill of your wives as a way to recreate a bond with any of you, and I promise not to use guilt to try to coax you back into close relationship with me if I were to feel rejected or overwhelmed because I find myself missing you both.

CHARGE *to Readers:*

Has there been divorce anywhere in your family? If so, even now, begin praying (it's never too early) and ask God to break this generational curse and spirit of divorce from your family. If not, ask God to sabotage the plans of the enemy and keep it away from your child(ren). Pray for your daughter's future husband. Pray that he will remain pure and undefiled. Pray that he will not have lustful eyes. Pray that the God of our fathers will be his source of strength even from his youth. Pray that he will love your daughter as God loves the church, willing to sacrifice his life for her. Pray that your daughter will align her marital and spousal expectations with God's so that she will not set him up to fail and cause turmoil in her marriage and home.

READER's *action plan for today:*

Write down ways you plan to assist your daughter and her husband and present them to God. Write down possible ways you know you could interfere in your child's marriage and present them to God. Ask Him, even now, to take those desires away.

1. _____

2. _____

3. _____

Amazing Love! How Can It Be?

This section captures the overwhelming gratitude in my heart to God just for who He is as my Father. Words inadequately describe the way I feel about His love and care for me. I have come to realize just how special I am to Him, and just how precious and valuable my life really is in light of eternity. May you catch a glimpse of His amazing and undying love for you.

Be encouraged and be blessed!

Your eyes saw my substance, being yet unformed. And in Your book they all were written, the days fashioned for me, when as yet there were none of them. How precious also are Your thoughts to me, O God! How great is the sum of them!

—*Psalm 139:16-17*

A Father Loves at All Times

My Heavenly Father,

I write You this love letter to express my gratitude and love for who You are and for what You have done and continue to do for me. I know my words cannot truly convey how thankful I am for all that You have sacrificed for me, for the love You have shown me when I was unlovable, and for forgiving me of my sins every day I sinned against You. Thank You, and I love You!

Thank You for sending Your son, Jesus Christ, to die for my sins. Thank You for sending the Holy Spirit to guide and direct my thoughts and actions and for never leaving my side. Thank You for sending Your heavenly angels to protect me. I know they are watching over me, walking by my side, and helping me through all of life's perplexities.

Thank You for all the blessings You have bestowed upon me. Thank You for the strength You have given me to go through each day and the courage to overcome my past hardships and pain. Thank You for loving me at my worst and darkest times and for promising NEVER TO LEAVE ME NOR FORSAKE ME. Thank You for being my perfect example. You have shown me how to forgive those who have hurt me. Thank You for all my experiences, both good and bad, because I am who I am because they have all influenced my character and shaped me into the woman I am today. Thank You for strategically placing different people in my life who loved me, nurtured my talent, cared for me, and helped me to be the woman I am today.

Thank You for all my family and friends. Thank You for ALWAYS blessing my family. Life wasn't and isn't perfect, but I have a wonderful supportive family who loves and cherishes me. And thanks for answering my prayers. I am beyond thankful and blessed to have my husband and children; my life is changed because of their love. Thank You for protecting my heart so that I could find and experience true love again. Thank You for preserving and protecting my mind, NEVER once letting me go because You love me so dearly. I am living proof that we can all be changed by the power of love.

Thank You for ALWAYS forgiving my sins. I know it breaks Your heart every time I go outside of Your will, but Your love is patient and longsuffering, not desiring that I should be lost. Thank You for guiding me along the path that reflects Your character despite my imperfections. Thank You for guiding and leading me toward the life You have purposed for me to live.

Thank You for teaching me how to trust blindly in simple childlike faith. Thank You for teaching and allowing me to walk in Your path of righteousness. Thank You for not allowing me to give up when I wanted to, reminding me that You are my refuge and strength, an ever-present help in trouble. Thank You for never giving up on me. Most of all, thank You for loving me before I was conceived in my mother's womb.

I am fully known and loved by You, and I love You because I know no other way of saying thank You. Thank You!

Your daughter,
Sherita

My Prayer

Father in Heaven, I thank You for who You are and that Courtney and I belong to You. I thank You for the promises that You have made concerning us and our union. Thank You that, in You, we can love each other totally and completely "for love is from God; and everyone who loves is born of God and knows God" (1 John 4:7). We thank You that You've given us marriage as a holy covenant with each other and as a means of reflecting our relationship with You. "Teach [us] Your ways, o LORD, that we may live according to Your truth! Grant [us] purity of heart, so that [we] may honor You." (Psalm 86:11)

Father, help us to be like-minded and of one spirit in valuing each other above ourselves. Your Word tells us, "Then make my joy complete by being like-minded, having the same love, being one in spirit and of one mind. "Do nothing out of selfish ambition or vain conceit. Rather, in humility value others above yourselves, not looking to your own interests but each of you to the interests of the others" (Philippians 2:2–4). Help us to look to You always in aiding us in the care of each other. May we never be too busy to love each other in the purity of our Father's love. For Your Word tells us, "Follow God's example, therefore, as dearly loved children and walk in the way of love, just as Christ loved us and gave Himself up for us as a fragrant offering and sacrifice to God" (Ephesians 5:1–2). May the love we have for each other stand worthy of emulation by our children and as a testimony to the world.

Lord, of ourselves, we cannot accomplish this. But You tell us in Your Word, "My grace is sufficient for You, for My power is made perfect in weakness" (2 Corinthians 2:9). Our hearts' desire is to honor and serve You, Lord, in spirit and in truth. We pray for a fresh awakening and renewal of Your Spirit's power within us, Father. "Create in [us] a pure heart, O God, and renew a steadfast spirit within [us]. Do not cast [us] from Your presence or take Your Holy Spirit from [us]" (Psalm 51:10–11), but rather let Your will be done in us.

Father, we commit our children to You. We stand on Your Word concerning them, "All Your children shall be taught by the Lord and great shall be their peace" (Isaiah 54:13). We will believe Your report concerning our offspring, Lord. We proclaim Your undisputed Word that "from everlasting to everlasting the Lord's love is with those who fear Him, and His righteousness with their children's children" (Psalm 103:17). We will rest in Your promise of blessings and multiplication for our lives as Your Word declares, "I will certainly bless You. I will multiply Your descendants beyond number, like the stars in the sky and the sand on the seashore. Your descendants will conquer the cities of their enemies" (Genesis 22:17).

You are "the Way, the Truth and the Life" (John 14:6). "Before the mountains were born or You brought forth the whole world, from everlasting to everlasting You are God" (Psalm 90:2). Your Word stands forever true, O Lord. Like Simon Peter, I declare, "Lord, to whom shall we go? You have the words of eternal life" (John 6:68). We rest safely in this blessed assurance, Lord, that Your promises for us are "Yes and amen" (2 Corinthians 1:20). We thank and praise You, O Lord, our Father.

In Jesus's name, amen.

"Who can find a virtuous woman? for her price is far above rubies. The heart of her husband doth safely trust in her, so that he shall have no need of spoil. She will do him good and not evil all the days of her life." (Proverbs 31:10–12)

"Train up a child in the way he should go and when he is old, he will not depart from it." (Proverbs 22:6)

About the Author

B orn and raised on the beautiful island of Jamaica, Sherita Thompson migrated to the United States in 2005 to complete her studies.

She holds dual master's degrees in Rehabilitation Counseling from the University of Maryland Eastern Shore and Counseling Psychology from Bowie State University.

An avid lover of sports, Sherita is passionate about track and field and football. She also takes great delight in teaching her children about the love of God, cooking, and baking, and she enjoys watching wholesome documentaries with her husband.

Sherita is the founder of They Changed Me, an online outreach ministry for women, whose goal is to encourage and nurture faith in God and inspire women to reach their highest and best potential on an individual level, at home, in their families, and in the world around them.

To subscribe, visit www.theychangedme.com.